Contents

Preface   iv

Introduction   1

Chapter One   Transport, transport trends and the economy   3
Chapter Two   Transport costs, negative externalities and
                 government regulation   16
Chapter Three   Resource allocation issues: investment in transport   32
Chapter Four   Market structures and competitive behaviour in
                 transport markets   49
Chapter Five   Traffic congestion and policies for combating
                 traffic congestion   76
Chapter Six   From transport economics to transport policies   93

Examination skills for transport economics   110
Conclusion   120
Index   121

Preface

Transport Economics justifiably continues to be one of the most popular titles in the SEB series. Its author, Professor Colin Bamford, is not only an acknowledged expert in the field but also a chief examiner with a leading awarding body and a very clear communicator.

This fully revised edition contains a number of new features and new information. Advice is provided on examination skills and there are some original questions and investigative tasks. The book takes into account recent developments in transport trends and transport policy. It also provides something that teachers and students of transport economics have long sought – a lucid description of the market structures operating in the transport sector.

The book should be essential reading for anyone studying for the OCR transport economics module and indeed, for any students studying A level business economics and transport economics at university level.

Susan Grant, Series Editor

Introduction

The first edition of this book was published in 1995. In the relatively short space of time between then and the publication of this fourth edition, much has changed in terms of the development of transport policies and the contribution of transport economists. This new edition takes into account these changes. It also includes a number of other changes and additions, such as:

- a list at the start of each chapter outlining what you will learn and a summary at the end of each chapter
- activities which provide topics for investigation
- a section on examination skills for transport economists
- a much revised chapter on market structures and competitive behaviour in transport markets
- updated statistics, figures and box items.

The approach throughout the text is to apply principles of economic analysis to a range of transport problems and issues, with a particular emphasis on micro-economics and market failure, set within their macro-economic context.

To keep up-to-date, students are strongly encouraged to read a quality newspaper – the transport issues featured in this book have an ever-increasing coverage in the national press. There is an excellent website for the Department for Transport (www.dft.gov.uk) which now contains policy statements, consultation documents and statistical information.

The book is a recommended text for OCR's transport economics module and will be of relevance to AQA and Edexcels' micro modules. The book is also likely to be useful to students taking the examinations and professional qualifications of the Chartered Institute of Logistics and Transport, both in the UK and elsewhere. Undergraduates taking modules in this subject will also find the book of introductory value.

Every edition of this book has benefited from the feedback I have received from students and teachers and I hope readers will find this new edition stimulating and informative.

1 Transport, transport trends and the economy

In this chapter, you will learn:
- what is meant by transport
- why the demand for transport is a derived demand
- the advantages and disadvantages of the main modes of transport
- how transport provision is organised in the UK
- how to analyse and interpret recent trends in the demand for transport
- how and why economists make forecasts of transport demand
- how to assess the economic importance of the transport sector in the UK economy.

Key words derived demand • forecast • infrastructure
mode of transport • supply chain • sustainability

What is transport?

All of us invariably need and use **transport** in our daily lives, whether it be to travel to school or college, to work or for leisure. Transport is also an essential part of the supply chain, providing the physical link between producers and consumers of fresh and manufactured goods. In both cases, the function of transport is that of facilitating movement. Therefore, the following definition is a good starting point:

Transport is the movement of people or goods for various personal and business reasons.

For the purpose of this book, this definition needs to be extended to cover the following:
- The means or **mode of transport** that is used. This covers the vehicle that is used to move people or goods and in general covers cars, buses, trains, aeroplanes, lorries, ships and so on.
- The way or **infrastructure** with which the vehicle is used, including roads, railway track, airspace, sea channels, as well as facilities such as stations, distribution centres and airports.

It is important from the outset that the scope of 'transport' is understood, as we shall see later. This is because:

- Decisions on modal choice are made by millions of consumers; decisions on infrastructure in contrast are in the main taken by the government, particularly in the case of roads.
- The day-to-day operation of the main modes of transport is very much in the hands of private companies and individuals. The government has a limited say through the subsidies that are paid to rail and to local bus passenger operators.

Transport modes and characteristics

Transport as a derived demand

At this stage, it is worth considering the nature of transport demand in the light of what has already been mentioned. To the economist, the demand for transport is a **derived demand**. This means that transport as a service or function is not demanded purely for what it is, but for what it can do. This general definition implies that people want transport because it enables them to do something, for example, businesses require goods transport in order to carry out activities within their **supply chain**.

Taking passenger transport first, the National Travel Survey provides considerable information on why people travel. The overall results of the most recent survey are shown in Table 1. Travel purposes are split into three main groups: work and education, which tend to result in very regular demand; shopping and personal business; and trips made for social and leisure purposes.

Excluding walking, the table indicates that:

- 84 per cent of all trips requiring transport are made by private car, either as the driver or as a passenger
- rail's main function is for the journey to work or in the course of business
- although local buses account for just eight per cent of trips, the bus is widely used for all types of trip.

Although not shown, many trips are only short walking trips, especially where the survey recorded all travel above 50 yards in length.

Factors affecting the demand for transport services

The derived demand for transport can be represented in the same general way as the demand for any given good or service. For passenger transport:

- Demand = f (Price, Price of substitutes, Income of passengers, Quality variables) (for a given mode)

Table 1: Trips[1] per person per year by main mode[2] and purpose: 2003

	Walk	Bicycle	Car driver	Car passenger	Motor-cycle	Other private	Local stage bus	Surface rail/under ground	Other public	All modes
Commuting/Business	13	6	113	17	2	1	12	10	2	181
Education/Escort education	51	1	23	25	–	4	11	1	1	117
Shopping	49	2	81	41	–	–	16	1	2	192
Other escort/personal business	38	1	92	51	–	1	8	1	2	194
Leisure	49	5	92	91	1	2	12	4	7	263
Other	39	–	–	–	–	–	–	–	–	39
All purposes	244	15	401	225	3	8	59	17	14	986

Source: **National Travel Survey**

Note:
[1] A trip is defined as a one way course of travel with a single main purpose.
[2] Main mode is that used for the longest part of the trip.

and for goods transport:

- Demand = f (Price, Price of substitutes, Speed/quality of service, Goods to be moved) (for a given mode)

Although the price charged is obviously important, as indeed is the price of substitutes, factors other than prices tend to be very important in determining the demand for all kinds of transport. Even so, the fares charged by bus and rail companies over the past decade have increased above the rate of inflation and above the change in costs of owning a car (see Table 2 on page 8). This could have influenced the modal choice of some passengers.

For passenger transport, the purpose of the trip is often important. Where travel is for personal reasons such as holidays or visiting friends and relatives, price is invariably an important consideration. This is less important where travel is for business reasons.

Case Study: Virgin trains

The introduction of 125mph trains between London and Manchester has triggered a big switch from air to rail travel on the route. Between March 2004 and March 2005, the number of people flying between the two destinations fell 12 per cent; at the same time, the number of people travelling by rail rose 37 per cent from 104 304 to 142 640, just 17 000 fewer than those travelling by air.

This is good news for Virgin and its partner on the franchise, Stagecoach. A spokesman for Virgin Trains commented 'This is only the start...by the end of the year we expect to have trains travelling at 125mph between London Euston and Glasgow'. The Pendolino experience though does not come cheap for customers. The cost of the two hour six minute trip from Manchester to London can cost as much as £187 return, although this is still over £100 cheaper than the lowest 'walk on' air fare.

Virgin and Stagecoach have invested heavily in new rolling stock and in the upgrading of the West Coast main line for which subsidy has been received. The likely outcome of the passenger growth though is that they will end up paying a 'premium' to run this franchise when new terms are negotiated with the government.

Source: Tracey Boles, The Business, 19/20 January 2005 (adaptation)

The recent successes of low-fare airlines in Europe and the USA has, in part, been due to the fares charged being affordable to people who would not otherwise have travelled. The same can be said about promotional fares on the railways – train operators are keen to see their seats occupied, hence fares that are set at, or a little above, marginal cost prices.

For private car travel, the position is more complicated. Car availability is a crucial variable in determining transport modal choice. For the vast majority of travellers, this tends to override all other considerations. As the next chapter shows though, car users tend to have a narrow view of the price they are paying, often thinking only in terms of the variable costs, fuel especially. When seen in these terms, the car is much more competitive than rail for all types of journey.

For freight transport, there are usually less decisions to be taken, mainly because of the goods that are to be moved and the timescale involved. For most inland transport, businesses have no choice other than to move their goods by road. The only choice they face is that of whether they use their own vehicles or whether they use a professional hauler or logistics contractor. For some goods though, a choice is available, for example between road and rail or between sea and air transport. In these cases, the type of product, its value and time sensitivity usually determine the mode of transport used.

So, modal characteristics can be very important in determining transport demand from a personal and business standpoint. Table 3 on page 9 gives a summary of these characteristics for the main modes of transport.

Equivalent information on trip purpose is not available for freight transport movements since most goods are carried in the course of business. Figure 1

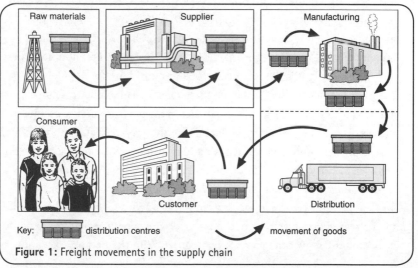

Figure 1: Freight movements in the supply chain

shows a stylised representation of the supply chain. The arrows on this figure show where freight transport is required, for example:

- in moving raw materials to be processed
- in moving manufactured goods to distribution centres
- in moving goods from a retailer's distribution centre to supermarkets for sale to consumers.

Table 2: Transport costs and retail prices, 1993–2003 (1993=100)

	Retail Prices Index	Private car costs	Rail fares	Bus fares
1993	100	100	100	100
1995	106.0	105.3	109.1	106.4
1997	112.0	114.3	115.8	114.3
1999	117.6	120.7	125.0	122.4
2001	123.2	124.6	132.0	132.6
2003	128.9	125.3	137.3	142.5

Source: Office for National Statistics, 2004

An overview of the supply of transport

The supply of transport involves two key elements as implied by the definition at the start of this chapter. These are:

- Infrastructure. This includes the provision of roads, railtrack, airports, ferry terminals, distribution centres and so on. For roads, virtually all provision is funded by central and local government, with a very small, though increasing, amount from the private sector (see Chapter 3). The same is broadly true for the provision of railway infrastructure. For all other types of infrastructure, it is the private sector's responsibility to provide.
- Transport vehicles. Used in the broadest sense, this includes private cars, goods vehicles, railway rolling stock, aeroplanes, ferries and container vessels. These are now provided largely by the private sector in the UK, either through individuals purchasing cars or businesses buying or leasing vehicles to carry out their work. In looking at the supply of transport, it should be recognised that decisions on supply are made by government and the private sector and involve complex processes. If anything, despite the increased use of transport, the issue of who supplies what has actually been simplified over the past 25 years or so. With the notable exception

Table 3: Characteristics of the main modes of transport

	Passenger transport
Road – private car	Flexible and convenient, providing door to door service, this mode is comfortable and easily used for carrying luggage and shopping. These attributes mean that it is widely used for all types of trip, although growing congestion can reduce its overall efficiency.
Road – bus	Widely used in London and other cities where car ownership levels are relatively low. Users are tied to the service provided, although the quality of the product has improved considerably. Not widely used for longer distance travel, this mode is not the general transport provider it once was.
Rail	Provides a speedy means of transport over middle to long distances, and into and out of congested cities and towns. Can carry large volumes of passengers in an environmentally acceptable way and is able to compete favourably with air on certain domestic routes (see *Air travellers switch to new Virgin trains* on page 4).
Air	High speeds over long distances make it highly attractive for business and leisure purposes. During inter-continental travel particularly, it often lacks comfort, but there are few realistic substitutes. It is the least sustainable of all modes.
Ferries	Limited to most short sea crossings. Can be expensive on a cost per kilometre basis.

	Freight transport
Road	Dominant mode, with clear advantages in terms of convenience, flexibility and quality of service. Heavier lorries have increased efficiency, and it is extensively used in retailing and where 'just-in-time' deliveries are required. It is not always the most sustainable mode and has a poor public image.
Rail	Comparative advantage over road for bulk shipments of basic products and for container traffic over longer distances. There are interchange limitations for certain types of potential traffic. Increasingly used for intra-EU loads.
Air	Clearly relevant for transporting time sensitive cargo such as mail and certain types of food products, but is cost restrictive.
Sea	Vast quantities of bulky goods, for example oil and containers, can be moved over longer distances where speed is not an important consideration.
Pipelines	Effective for transporting oil, bulk liquids and powder.

of roads and aspects of rail provision, the responsibility for the supply of transport lies firmly with the private sector.

Recent trends in the demand for transport

Figures 2 and 3 show how the demand for passenger and freight transport has changed since 1980. Before identifying the most important trends, it is worth considering the units used, namely 'billion passenger kilometres' and 'billion tonne kilometres'. These compound measures are indicative of the definition of transport given at the start of the chapter, namely that demand has to be seen in terms of both volume and distance travelled.

Figure 2 for passenger transport shows the following:

- The overall demand for passenger travel has increased consistently over the period shown; the rate of increase in demand though has fallen since around 1990.
- In 2003, 85 per cent of all domestic passenger travel was by private car.
- Of the remaining modes, the demand for rail travel has increased since privatisation in 1995, although rail's market share has remained at about six per cent of the total.
- Travel by bus and coach has been relatively stable in recent years with total demand being about what it was at the time of deregulation in 1986.

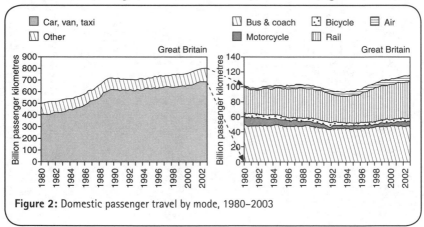

Figure 2: Domestic passenger travel by mode, 1980–2003

The main trends for freight transport are shown in Figure 3:

- The total demand for freight transport has increased by over 42 per cent from 1980 to 2003.
- Most of this increase has been for road transport.
- The demand for rail freight transport has increased by over 40 per cent since privatisation while its market share has increased to 10 per cent of all goods moved.

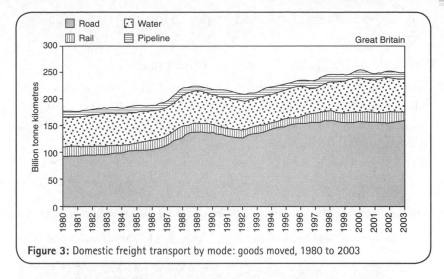

Figure 3: Domestic freight transport by mode: goods moved, 1980 to 2003

- The data for water transport is made up almost entirely of coastal shipping movements.
- The total demand has fluctuated in recent years and is dependent to some extent upon the wellbeing of the economy.

The trends shown in Figures 2 and 3 have particular significance for national transport policy (see Chapter 6). There is some evidence of increased **sustainability**, particularly for freight transport (see *We're better than ever!*). For both passenger and freight transport, in recent years, the rate of increase in demand has been below the rate of increase in real GDP. While this is

'We're better than ever!'

The road haulage industry is getting smarter and becoming increasingly efficient, according to the Freight Transport Association (FTA), the leading industry trade group for providers and consumers of transport services. The basis of the claim is that between 1998 and 2004, GDP increased on average by three per cent per year; over the same period, the amount of goods moved by large vehicles was unchanged.

The FTA believes that the introduction of 44 tonne vehicles in early 2001 is the main reason for this, producing benefits for the industry, its consumers and the environment. On this evidence, the historic link between GDP and road transport appears to have been broken.

Source: Freight, July 2005 (adaptation)

encouraging, total demand and hence congestion levels are increasing (see Chapter 5).

Forecasts of transport demand and their use

It may seem from a cursory glance at Figures 2 and 3 that **forecasting** future traffic levels using trends is a relatively easy task. This is, however, not the case and over the years, despite an increased level of sophistication, traffic forecasts have been shown to be inaccurate.

Table 4 shows some of the most recent forecasts that were made to coincide with the 'Future of Transport' consultation document (see Chapter 6 for details).

Table 4: % forecasted traffic growth on all types of road in England (Year 2000 base)

	2010	2015	2025
Cars	26	29	37
Light goods vehicles	39	54	74
Rigid goods vehicles	-1	1	6
Articulated goods vehicles	23	33	45
Passenger service vehicles	-1	-1	-1
All vehicles	26	31	40

Source: Department for Transport, 2004

In building up these forecasts, estimates were made of traffic on different types of road. For private car traffic, the forecasts were above the average shown for rural areas and slightly below the average in urban areas. For bus travel, traffic levels in London were expected to grow by 18 per cent to 2010 and then stabilise; elsewhere the decline was estimated to be between three and five per cent. Because of the uncertainty, high and low forecasts were also made.

Forecasting future road traffic levels is extremely difficult due to the wide range of factors that have to be taken into account. These include population and employment growth, household income and GDP growth, fuel costs, the numbers of people holding driving licences and the extent of additional roadspace provision and investment in the road network. Looking at all of these, and the uncertainties involved, it is easy to see why traffic forecasting is fraught with difficulty, even over a short period of time.

Traffic forecasts have two main purposes:

- Firstly, they address the need to be able to plan ahead, in particular for transport planners to have a fair idea as to the broad level of supply that is required to meet future needs.
- Secondly, forecasts can give an indication of the effectiveness of transport policies, at both a national and a local level.

It must be stressed that in both cases, they can only provide a pointer due to the forecasting problems involved.

The economic importance of the transport sector in the UK economy

It should be clear from what has been covered so far in this chapter, that the transport sector is an essential part of the UK economy, vital for business and personal well-being. Transport serves to allow supply chains to function effectively and for individuals to travel to work and carry out their lives in a meaningful way. This might seem obvious, yet in many respects, transport is often taken for granted and it is not until it fails, that we step back and realise where we would be without the transport sector.

More specifically:

- In 2004, almost one million people, or around five per cent of the working population, were directly employed in transport industries.
- Almost as many again, approximately 900 000, were employed in other types of transport related work.
- In 2003/04 in England, central and local government spent almost £15 000 million on capital and current transport expenditure – an estimated six per cent of total government spending.
- In 2003/04, the typical household spent around £60 per week on various types of transport services.

Summary

On completion of this chapter, you have learnt that:

- the demand for transport is a derived demand
- each of the main modes of transport has its own characteristics; in turn these can be used to explain some of the recent changes and trends in the demand for transport
- except for roads, the organisation of the supply of transport services largely lies with the private sector
- forecasting the future demand for transport, road in particular, is very difficult
- transport has a very important function within the modern day UK economy.

Useful websites

Department for Transport, www.dft.gov.uk

Chapter 1 of the 'Future of Transport' white paper provides a concise analysis of the importance of the transport function in the UK economy.

Activities

Topics for investigation

1. Go back to Figures 2 and 3. See what similar information you are able to find on passenger and freight transport trends in:

    a) another major developed EU country such as France or Germany

    b) an emerging economy such as Malaysia, China or Poland. Make a few notes on the similarities and differences.

Exam-style practice questions

Essay questions

1. Transport services such as local bus, rail and road haulage are mainly provided by the private sector, although provision can in part be influenced by government policy.

a) Explain the main factors affecting the supply of transport services for a transport mode of your choice   (10)

b) Discuss the factors that determine whether a manufacturer should use road or rail transport for the distribution of its goods.   (15)

(OCR Module 2885, June 2004)

Data response question

Study the information in the chart below.

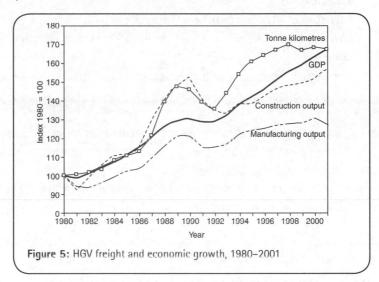

Figure 5: HGV freight and economic growth, 1980–2001

a) Explain why the demand for transport by the manufacturing and construction industries is a derived demand.   (4)

b) Compare the likely demand for transport for manufacturing and construction since 1992.   (6)

c) Comment upon the changing relationship between GDP growth and tonne kilometres demanded over the period shown in the graph.   (10)

2 Transport costs, negative externalities and government regulation

In this chapter, you will learn:

- how the costs of transport operations can be split into fixed costs and variable costs
- how economists classify the costs associated with transport use
- how increased transport use leads to negative externalities and market failure
- how governments can use indirect taxation and subsidies to regulate transport use.

Key words allocative efficiency • barrier to entry • external costs fixed costs • hypothecated • load factor • negative externalities positive externalities • price inelastic • private costs semi-fixed costs • shadow price • social costs • social equity subsidy • variable costs

The costs of transport operation

The costs of operating any type of transport vehicle (in the loosest sense) can be divided into two main types:

- **Fixed costs.** These are independent of the use made or output derived from using a transport vehicle and as such they cannot be changed in the short run.
- **Variable costs.** These vary with the use made or output derived from using a transport vehicle and while they can be varied in the short run, by definition, they must be paid in full if a transport operation is to remain in business.

A third type of cost, **semi-fixed** costs, can also be recognised in most types of transport operation. These are costs that are incurred once a transport operation decides to operate a particular service. For example, an airline has to incur certain costs when it operates a particular flight. These include crew costs, certain fuel costs and landing charges, all of which are incurred irrespective of the number of passengers on board. Another example is in the case of a road haulage company that might be delivering goods in a situation where the vehicle is not loaded to its full capacity. The driver's wage, some maintenance and fuel costs can be regarded as semi-fixed costs.

All of these costs are **private costs** in the sense that they are incurred and have to be paid for by the user or provider of transport services. In many types of transport operation, the fixed costs are high in relation to total costs. This can present an effective **barrier to entry** to new firms wishing to set up in business in a transport market (see Chapter 4).

Table 1 below shows the cost structure in the above terms for the main modes of transport. The 'other costs' column contains costs that are usually fixed and for businesses, a contribution has to be included for costing purposes.

Table1: Cost structure of the main transport modes

Mode	Fixed costs	Variable costs	Other costs
Private car	Purchase costs, insurance, road tax, depreciation	Fuel, maintenance	
Large goods vehicles	Capital costs, licences, insurance, depreciation	Fuel, maintenance, drivers' wages	Depot costs, administration
Rail	Track charges, capital costs/ lease costs, depreciation	Fuel, maintenance, labour	Interchange costs, administration, depot costs
Air	Capital costs, depreciation, landing charges	Fuel, maintenance, labour, in-flight services	

Figure 1 shows the typical operating costs of a short haul airline. This clearly indicates the high percentage of fixed costs in relation to total costs, even allowing for problems of allocating semi-fixed costs. This cost structure means that in order to survive, an airline must have an average **load factor** of around 65 per cent. For low-fare airlines, the figure is even higher at 80–85 per cent.

Classification of transport costs

Economists classify costs into three types:

- **Private costs.** These are costs that are paid directly by the user for the use of resources. For transport, this would include the cost of operating

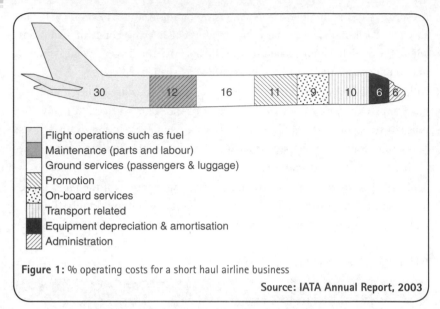

Flight operations such as fuel
Maintenance (parts and labour)
Ground services (passengers & luggage)
Promotion
On-board services
Transport related
Equipment depreciation & amortisation
Administration

Figure 1: % operating costs for a short haul airline business

Source: IATA Annual Report, 2003

a transport vehicle, the cost of constructing a new stretch of road and so on. For such costs, a market price is usually available.

- **External costs.** These are costs that have to be indirectly paid for by third parties and can arise as a consequence of the way in which transport is used. Typical examples are the additional costs that are incurred by road users as a result of increased congestion or the environmental costs arising from the increased demand for most forms of mechanised transport. In most cases, it is not possible to calculate a market price so the cost has to be imputed, that is, a **shadow price** is estimated.

- **Social costs.** This is the sum of private costs and external costs. An optimum allocation of resources occurs where the users of transport are paying the true cost or social cost. This optimum does not occur in many transport markets – the private costs do not always fully reflect the social costs and as a consequence, the market is failing to allocate resources in an efficient way. As a result, the benefit that an individual receives from using a particular form of transport is out of line with the cost to society. As the next section indicates, this is an increasing problem in most transport markets.

Negative externalities of increased transport use

Chapter 1 analysed recent trends in the demand for transport in Britain. For the majority of the population, notably car owners, the increase in vehicle ownership and use has brought about many benefits and has had a profound effect on our lives and lifestyles. The same can also be said for the increase in air transport use, particularly for holiday purposes. This has though come at a cost – increased use of transport pollutes the environment and through CO_2 emissions, is a major contributor to the increase in greenhouse gases and the longer term effect of global warming.

The blunt truth is that increased transport use results in many **negative externalities**. These include:

- Noise pollution. The noise from road traffic produces a level of pitch that over time becomes unwelcome to the human ear. Prolonged exposure can disrupt lifestyle, increase stress and make it difficult to concentrate or relax. The noise from aircraft can be particularly disruptive as the millions of people who live under the flight paths to major airports will readily confirm.

- Atmospheric pollution. Road and air traffic directly produce CO_2 emissions and are also major users of scarce oil resources (see Chapter 6). Improvements to the design of vehicles, fuel efficiency initiatives and various other means have helped to cut back on total emissions. Rail transport also generates pollution, particularly where the electricity being used is generated from coal power stations.

- Visual intrusion. This is the term used to describe a situation where, through providing transport facilities, there is a devaluation of the urban or rural landscape. In many towns and cities, this is the case, with historical buildings invariably looking out of place when surrounded by a sea of cars.

- Blight. This is a type of negative externality that can be caused through unsympathetic local planning or where there might be uncertainty over whether a new transport project is going to go ahead.

- Community severance. Providing new roads, especially in urban areas, has sometimes resulted in whole communities being torn apart and physically divided.

- Accidents. Road traffic accidents are very costly to individuals and to the economy due to the serious injuries and loss of life that can occur. Over the years economists have developed a methodology for costing accidents (see page 21). Reduced accident levels provide an important benefit in the appraisal of most new road schemes (see Chapter 3). In contrast, accident rates for other modes of transport are very low relative to road.

Another very important negative externality associated with increased traffic use is that of traffic congestion. This is a very important area of study in transport economics (see Chapter 5).

In all cases, as a consequence of negative externalities, external costs arise as one group in the community has indirectly imposed costs on another group. The economics underpinning this state of affairs is shown in Figure 2. As this makes clear, there is an allocatively inefficient situation as the social costs are greater than the private costs. Hence, the price that is being paid in the market is lower than the social optimum.

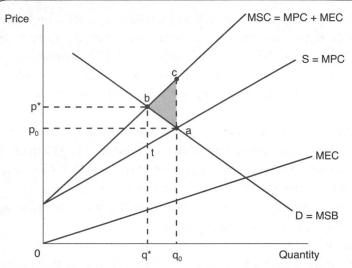

(MEC = marginal external costs; MPC = marginal private costs; MSC = marginal social costs)

Allocative efficiency is achieved where MSC = MSB.

The MSC schedule is the vertical sum of MPC and MEC.

The private market extends production to q_0, where D = S,

but for each unit between q^* and q_0, MSC is greater than MSB.

These units should not be produced.

The deadweight loss from their production is given by the shaded triangle *abc*.

Consequently:

Social costs   >   Private costs

Quantity demanded is higher than optimum.

Price paid by users is lower than optimum.

REMEDY: INCREASED TAXATION SO THAT MSC = MSB

(a green tax)

Figure 2: Private and social costs divergence

The costs of road traffic accidents

The benefit arising from a reduction in road traffic accidents is an important element in the cost-benefit appraisal of new trunk road schemes (see Chapter 3). The economic underpinning is that over the years economists have developed a methodology for putting a monetary value on the cost of road accidents. As well as the 'casualty cost' of accidents, estimates have also been made of the cost of negative externalities with respect to damaged property, insurance administration and police time. In practice, the cost estimates are very complex and vary depending on the type of road, the speed of vehicles involved and the degree of severity. Tables 2 and 3 show the latest average costs per casualty and per accident at 2002 prices and values.

Table 2: The average cost per casualty in 2002

	£ per casualty
Fatal casualty	1 249 890
Serious casualty	140 450
Slight casualty	10 830

The largest item is that given for the human costs of an accident – this is a measure of the loss of income and the personal distress and suffering that arises as a consequence of an accident. The younger the victim and the higher the person's income, the greater the actual cost of an accident. An estimate is also included for the loss of output to the economy.

Table 3: Cost per accident (£)

	Insurance administration	Damage to property			Police cost		
		Urban	Rural	M'way	Urban	Rural	M'way
Fatal accident	230	5 977	10 136	12 894	1 463	1 387	2 030
Serious accident[1]	143	3 203	4 620	11 002	122	341	320
Slight accident[2]	87	1 890	3 063	5 566	44	44	44
Damage only	42	1 352	2 019	1 941	3	3	3

Note:
[1] A serious accident is one where a casualty requires A and E treatment involving a stay of two nights or more.
[2] A slight accident is one where a casualty requires A and E treatment with or without an overnight stay.

Source: COBA Manual, Department for Transport, 2005 (adaptation)

The true cost of road traffic accidents

Road users currently inflict costs on society through road accidents, noise, air pollution and congestion. In 1999, road users paid around £32 billion in total road taxation – fuel duty, vehicle excise duty and VAT – yet the total road expenditure was close to just £6 billion, representing a substantial surplus of over £26 billion[1]. This surplus went into the Exchequer to fund other forms of government spending. Some groups might call this 'highway robbery' or 'milking the motorist'. An alternative view is that this surplus can be viewed as compensation that is paid to society to make up for the damage that is caused through the negative externalities associated with road use.

Research by the Adam Smith Institute has estimated the external costs of road use to be £25 billion at 1999 prices, the equivalent of 5.4 pence per vehicle kilometre. A disaggregation of how this estimate was derived is shown in Table 4.

Table 4: The external costs of road use

	£bn	% Total
Congestion	18	72
Accidents	3	12
Air pollution	3	12
Noise pollution	1	4
Total	25	100

The implication from this is that on average, road users are paying the right level of taxation. This is though an over-simplification, as certain categories of road user pay far too much while others pay far too little. For example:

- *users of goods vehicles impose higher external costs than car users, particularly with respect to pollution and congestion*

- *vehicles used in the central area of towns and cities during peak times impose the highest external costs*

- *vehicles used in rural areas and on motorways impose the least external costs, well below the average.*

The message is very clear: a tremendous imbalance exists in the different external costs that road users impose on each other and on the community as a whole.

Note: [1] In 2004, road users paid around £42 billion in various forms of taxation, while expenditure on roads was about £15 billion. The surplus was £27 billion, only marginally above the estimate made for 1999.

Source: The Road from Inequity, Adam Smith Institute, 2000 (adaptation)

The environmental costs of the tomato on your plate

It is rather surprising to believe that it takes less energy to import tomatoes from Spain than to grow them in the UK. This is one of the conclusions of a report commissioned by the Department of the Environment, Food and Rural Affairs. The reason of course is that the climate in Spain is warmer and no heating is required to grow tomatoes even out of season. This more than compensates for the energy used in distributing tomatoes to UK retailers.

Over the past 50 years or so, the food we consume has been travelling longer distances or 'food miles' as it is sometimes known. This is the result of the increased globalisation of the food industry (see Chapter 6), the trend towards bigger farms, the centralisation of retail distribution networks and the growth of out-of-town shopping by car.

This trend is not without its costs. Food transport is a significant and growing source of road congestion, road accidents, noise and pollution. It has been estimated that the external costs of food transport are £9 billion per year; more than half of this is attributed to road congestion. The cost of accidents involving vehicles transporting food is estimated at £2 billion. Carbon dioxide emissions from food vehicles increased by 12 per cent from 1992 to 2002, a consequence of the continuing increase in the food miles travelled.

Source: Daily Telegraph, 15 July 2005 (adaptation)

Putting a monetary value upon negative externalities is a difficult task, not least because some of the variables involved (e.g. cost of a good night's sleep, cost of clean, unpolluted air) do not have a market price. Economists have therefore sought to develop a methodology for calculating such instances. As Table 4 shows, a relatively recent study by the Adam Smith Institute has estimated that the costs of negative externalities associated with road transport are around £25 billion per year. 72 per cent of this estimate is accounted for by the external cost of traffic congestion (see also Chapter 5). An even more recent study is that which has been made of the external costs that are a consequence of food being transported throughout Britain. (See Figure 3). Broadly speaking, this study has some observations that are in common with those from the Adam Smith Institute. Its main conclusion is that the local sourcing of food is likely to generate less food miles compared to the present methods of distribution. This is seen by many as a way of moving towards a more sustainable transport policy (see also Chapter 6).

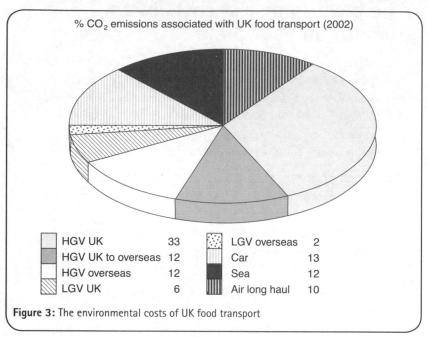

% CO_2 emissions associated with UK food transport (2002)

HGV UK	33	LGV overseas	2
HGV UK to overseas	12	Car	13
HGV overseas	12	Sea	12
LGV UK	6	Air long haul	10

Figure 3: The environmental costs of UK food transport

The use of indirect taxation and subsidies

As shown earlier in this chapter, in 2004, road users paid around £42 billion in various forms of indirect taxation such as fuel duty, VAT, Vehicle Excise Duty, goods vehicle licences and so on. In return, central and local government spent £15 billion on new roads and on road maintenance. As argued earlier, this might seem about right when all of the costs of road transport are taken into account, but not all would agree. The 'road lobby', consisting of trade associations such as the Freight Transport Association, motoring organisations and road construction companies, argue that road users are taxed far too heavily and that more should be spent on road maintenance and new road schemes.

The original idea behind the Road Fund Tax (Vehicle Excise Duty as it is now known) was that the revenue from it was to be ploughed back into providing facilities for road users who have paid the tax. In other words, it was to be **hypothecated** into providing better infrastructure for road users. This is no longer the case. Road users have long been seen as a valuable source of tax revenue for governments, with much of the revenue being used to fund other public sector expenditure such as education, health and social security.

In April 2005 the average price of a litre of unleaded petrol was 85.4 pence. The total tax, fuel duty and VAT, was 59.8 pence (70 per cent of the price). Fuel tax alone raised almost £25 billion in the financial year 2004/05. After the Netherlands, the UK has the most expensive fuel in the EU, and the price of fuel has become a major political issue following the fuel protests in the autumn of 2000, when the country virtually came to a halt when oil refineries were blockaded.

In theory, as the price of fuel rises through increased indirect taxation, the demand for fuel should fall. This is shown in Figure 4. So, if the government were to increase fuel tax, this would shift the supply curve to the left resulting in an increase in price from P_1 to P_2 and a resulting fall in demand from Q_1 to Q_2. In practice, this effect does not occur to the same degree indicated in the figure. The demand for fuel is highly **price inelastic** (even more so than indicated on Figure 4); it is an essential good with no real substitutes, so when fuel tax is increased, there is little change in the quantity of fuel that is purchased. Superficially, therefore, increasing the indirect tax on fuel could be seen as a way of recouping the cost of the negative externalities associated with increased road use. For the political reasons stated earlier, though, the government has been forced to pull back, for the time being, from introducing any major increases in the price of fuel as a means of compensating for the cost of negative externalities.

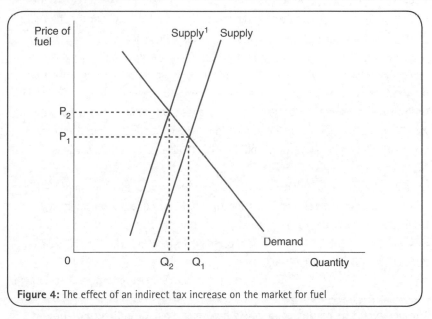

Figure 4: The effect of an indirect tax increase on the market for fuel

Figure 2 on page 20 showed that the most effective way of combating negative externalities was to introduce a green tax. The proposed national road user charge can be seen in these terms, if it is ever implemented (see Chapter 5).

A further interesting form of indirect taxation is the car plate tax which has been introduced in Shanghai (see *The China crisis*). This seeks to restrict the quantity of new vehicles by imposing a monthly quota on licences. Would-be purchasers of new vehicles have to put in a bid for a car plate before they can purchase. In a crude way, this tax increases the cost of vehicle use to those who are successful in the auction process.

Another example, working on the same basic principle, is the proposal to introduce an emissions trading scheme for air transport. The principle behind it is that air travellers in the EU would have to pay an extra charge or tax to help offset damage to the environment caused by pollutants emitted during the flight (see Chapter 6). The revenue from the charge could be used to pay for schemes that reduce carbon use, for example tree planting. If implemented, this tax would increase the price of all flights, particularly those with low-fare airlines. Ryanair, Europe's largest low-cost airline, is not in favour as might be expected. Most scheduled carriers though, support the idea.

Case Study: The China crisis

By 2031, China would have 1.1 billion cars if it matches current trends of growth. This would be bigger than the present world fleet of 800 million; if uncontrolled, the growth of China's CO_2 emissions would dwarf any cuts that are made by the rest of the world, making China the top emitter of greenhouse gases in the world.

Beijing is one of the world's most polluted cities. There are around 2.5 million cars, a number increasing by 1000 a day as the emerging middle classes turn their backs on bicycles and a public transport system that serves just a fraction of the city. Trucks with dodgy exhaust systems and traffic to the thousands of construction sites, many for the 2008 Olympic Games, exacerbate the situation. There is so much dust in the air that no one leaves their car windows open and the city's thousands of cyclists need face masks to protect themselves.

The authorities in Beijing are reluctant to do anything to stem this environmental disaster. In contrast, the authorities in Shanghai have introduced a Singapore-style bidding process whereby each month, anyone wishing to buy a new car must purchase a car plate in a monthly auction. To be successful, a typical bid is likely to be between 30–35 000 RMB (about £3000–3500).

Source: Independent, 19 October 2005

Irrespective of its nature, economists favour the use of indirect taxation as a means of correcting market failure for two reasons. Firstly, it allows the market to operate and secondly, in so doing, it internalises to the user the cost of negative externalities. In the longer term, this can result in a better allocation of resources since those affected by an indirect tax can seek to reduce their tax liability.

A second form of intervention in transport markets is where central or local government provides a **subsidy**. Like indirect taxation, it can take many forms – in all cases though, it is a payment made to suppliers or consumers to reduce the market price of the good or service. This is shown in Figure 5. Where transport operators, for example, receive a subsidy payment, the effect is to shift the supply curve to the right. This results in a fall in the market price and a consequent increase in the quantity that is demanded as well as supplied. The effect of introducing a subsidy is not only to reduce the price; it also leads to an increase in revenue from consumers as more people will be using the service to travel.

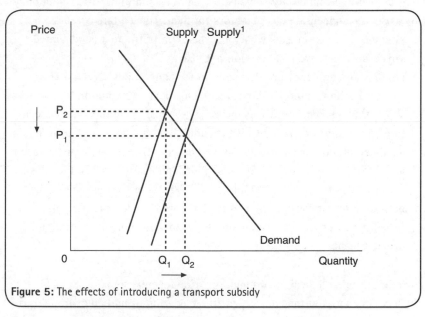

Figure 5: The effects of introducing a transport subsidy

The main economic argument for subsidies is where such a payment will produce **positive externalities**. In such instances there is an external benefit to the community arising out of the payment that has been made. For example, a subsidy paid to support local rail services could result in reduced road traffic congestion in a particular town or city. A second more historical argument for transport subsidies is on the grounds of **social equity**. By subsidising transport fares, certain groups in the community who would otherwise be unable to travel can now do so, enhancing their accessibility to work and leisure opportunities.

In the UK, the government subsidises bus and rail services in various ways. For bus services, this support includes:

- Local authority support for socially necessary services. Following deregulation, local authorities have a duty to secure socially necessary bus services that are not provided commercially by the private bus operators (see Chapter 4). Over £200 million a year is provided and this supports an estimated 15 per cent of all bus services outside of London. The decision on whether to subsidise is left to the discretion of the local authorities.

- Bus Services Operators Grant. This is a rebate of 80 per cent to bus operators of the duty paid on diesel fuel. It cost around £350 million in 2003.

- Concessionary fares. Since 2001, local authorities have had a statutory requirement to provide at least half fares and a free bus pass to certain groups in the community such as the over 60s and under 18s. The money is used to compensate bus operators for their reduced fare revenue although there is some clawback for the extra traffic that is generated. This costs a massive £500 million per year.

- Funding through Transport for London for London bus services. The Greater London Authority currently spends over £600 million a year in supporting bus services. This subsidy is designed to fill the gap between fare box income and the cost of providing the services as set out in tender documentation. Since 2002, income from the congestion charge has been an important source of additional support and has resulted in the subsidy increasing from around £200 million in 2001. Some of this subsidy has been used to purchase new buses for London's franchised operators.

- Other, including rural bus grants and support for innovative rural and urban schemes.

For rail, central and local government provide revenue support for local rail services as part of the contract for the tendering of particular franchises (See Chapter 4). Support has also been provided for capital projects such as upgrading the West Coast Main Line (see Chapter 6).

As with indirect taxation, subsidies work through the market mechanism and, in the case of revenue support and concessionary fares, provide immediate benefit for those using the service. Unlike indirect taxation though, aspects of subsidy provision are more controversial. For example, a common complaint is that subsidies are untargeted in so far as where a service is subsidised, all passengers benefit from the subsidy irrespective of income or need. A second issue is that for bus services especially, too much is left to the discretion of local politicians. In some parts of the country, the attitude towards subsidy is rather negative. A final criticism is that the decision to subsidise is often based on limited evidence of need and limited evidence that other positive externalities are being generated.

Summary

On completion of this chapter you have learnt:

- how transport costs are classified and of the significance of this structure in transport operations
- why the true costs of transport use invariably exceed the private costs
- that it is often difficult to put a monetary value on the costs of all of the negative externalities associated with the increased use of transport
- why the use of indirect taxation and subsidies can be an effective way of correcting market failure in transport markets.

Useful websites

Adam Smith Institute www.adamsmith.org.uk

Royal Commission on Environmental Pollution www.rcep.org.uk

Activities

Topics for investigation

1. Obtain information on the costs of operating a large 44 tonne goods vehicle.

   a) Divide these costs into fixed costs and variable costs.

   b) Use this information to explain why it is very important for the owner of a 44 tonne goods vehicle to use it efficiently.

Exam-style practice questions

Data response question – Heathrow's fifth terminal

Following a major planning enquiry, it was recommended that a fifth terminal be built at Heathrow in the national economic interest and to keep London as a world financial centre. The report stated that strict controls would be required to prevent unacceptable noise and pollution, and above all, Terminal 5 would not lead to a third runway being constructed.

The report also recognised that there was widespread public distrust of government policy on aviation. This is because the government had abandoned its policy that a fifth terminal should not be permitted and that the number of flights should be limited. When Terminal 4 was approved, on condition that a fifth terminal would not be built, a limit of 300 000 flights a year was imposed. This has been ignored and the number of flights had reached 438 000 flights a year by the time the Terminal 5 enquiry closed.

Terminal 5 will cater for an extra 30 million passengers a year, adding to Heathrow's existing capacity of 60 million. However, this increase would not be enough to cater for the projected demand of 170 million air passengers a year in the South East by 2016, even if by then 40 million are using Gatwick, 15 million, Stansted and 10 million, Luton.

Yet Heathrow cannot compete with Charles de Gaulle, Schiphol and Frankfurt airports without the high standards of passenger comfort and services that will be provided at Terminal 5. The terminal will make a substantial contribution to the national economy, to the continued success of London as a financial centre and to the UK's ability to attract inward investment.

Costs

- The new terminal has been approved subject to clear and specific controls on aircraft noise and on night flights. There is a long-term objective of removing the need for night flights.

- The new terminal will result in increases in air pollutants around Heathrow because of more aircraft movements and larger planes. Steps will be taken to limit the impact by restricting the number of landings that involve flying over the heavily populated areas of West London.

- The risk of a major air crash involving many casualties on the ground raises questions about the future role of Heathrow.

- There will also be ecological damage. The construction will be visually intrusive but the new terminal will be a light, elegant construction to offset this.

- Increased congestion on road and rail links around Heathrow will result in the need to build new links to the airport.

Fairer Taxation

It has been argued that the airline industry does not pay its fair share of taxes in comparison to other modes of transport. It should be compelled to pay a much-needed tax on aviation fuel and perhaps an emissions tax to reflect the cost of additional environmental pollutants.

Source: Paul Brown, The Guardian, November 21, 2001 (adaptation)

1. State and explain:

   a) two external costs

   b) two external benefits
   that are likely to occur when Terminal 5 is operational.   (6)

2. Comment upon some of the problems you might have in putting a monetary value on these external costs and benefits.   (4)

3. Draw a diagram to show the likely effect on the market for air travel of a new tax on aviation fuel or a new emissions tax.   (4)

4. Discuss whether these new taxes might correct the misallocation of resources associated with the increased use of air transport.   (6)

Essay questions

1. Comment upon whether all Londoners are happy with the increased subsidy that is being provided for bus services in London.   (25)

2. Discuss the advantages and disadvantages of subsiding local suburban railway services.   (25)

3 Resource allocation issues: investment in transport

In this chapter, you will learn:
- why and how resources are allocated in transport
- about the respective roles of the public and private sectors in resource allocation decisions
- why the private sector is having an increasingly important role in funding transport investment, particularly through the Private Finance Initiative
- how the government uses cost-benefit analysis to allocate resources in transport and why this method of appraisal has some limitations
- about the different criteria that are applied by the private and public sectors in making investment decisions in transport.

> **Key words** cost-benefit analysis • economic problem
> investment • net present value • non-excludability • non-rivalry
> Private Finance Initiative • public good • quasi-public good

The resource allocation problem in transport

A study of transport economics is inevitably concerned with a whole range of transport problems and issues. This will become very clear as you progress through the next three chapters. Most, if not all, of these problems involve issues of resource allocation, namely that the needs of transport are in certain respects unlimited, yet there are only limited resources that can realistically be allocated to them. This is particularly true when dealing with the responsibilities of the public sector. Transport is therefore a very clear example of an **economic problem**.

Typical of the decisions that involve the public sector are:
- whether a new stretch of motorway should be built
- whether a historic town would benefit from the construction of a new ring road
- if funding should be provided for a new attractive light rail system
- whether it is a good idea to subsidise local rail and bus services.

Over the last 15–20 years, the private sector has had an increasing role to play in some resource allocation decisions. Deregulation and privatisation, for instance, have provided private companies with the opportunity to operate and invest heavily in transport (see Chapter 4). The sale of the UK's airports to the privately owned British Airports Authority has put the responsibility for funding airport development firmly in their hands, albeit with government involvement from a strategic standpoint (see Table 1). The M6 Toll Road that opened in 2004 is the first of its kind in so far as all funding has been from private sector sources. Increasingly, as the 10-year transport plan shows, the government is looking to the private sector as a partner in increasing the total resources that are being allocated to transport (see Chapter 6). The **Private Finance Initiative** has had a particular role to play in this respect.

Over the past 15–20 years the total resources going into transport have increased substantially due to the involvement of the private sector. (**Investment** in the purchase of cars and road goods vehicles has also increased but this is excluded from the scope of this chapter.) Typically, the public sector has allocated around six per cent of all government spending to transport. Table 1 shows in broad terms the total investment in transport infrastructure in the financial year 2003/04.

Excluding the general increase in private sector investment, the main changes over the past decade or so are as follows:

- Road investment has increased substantially since 1998/99 although it remains at the same level as in the early 1990s.
- Private sector road investment was substantially higher prior to the opening of the M6 Toll Road.
- Total investment in national rail infrastructure is almost three times as much as in 1993/94, prior to privatisation, while investment in rail rolling stock is up by one fifth and is now mainly the responsibility of the private sector.
- Total investment in airports and air traffic control has increased by almost 300 per cent since 1993/94 and is now largely the responsibility of the private sector.

Table 1: Investment in transport, 2003/04 (£ million, outturn prices[1])

	£m
Road infrastructure	
– public sector	4 191
– private sector	40
Rail infrastructure	
– National Rail[2]	4 722
– other[3]	464
Rail rolling stock[4]	
– National Rail	774
– other	147
Airports and air traffic control	
– public sector	70
– private sector	1 384

Notes:

[1] Final or outcome prices. These are particularly relevant for capital projects that exceed budget.

[2] Refers to the national rail network and is mainly investment by Network Rail in track renewals, electrification and signalling, although some private sector investment is included.

[3] Includes public and private sector investment in all other rail based transport systems including light rail.

[4] Mainly private sector investment for the national rail network and other rail based transport systems.

Source: Transport Statistics, Department for Transport, 2005 edition (adaptation)

In general terms, transport investment has certain common, inherent characteristics:

- Most forms of transport investment involve vast sums of capital expenditure.
- Any appraisal of new investment, especially in infrastructure, is made over a long time period; 30 years is typical for a new stretch of road and in the case of major projects, it could be as much as 50 years.
- On account of the above, transport investment involves many risks and uncertainties, particularly in the case of public transport infrastructure projects.
- Cost escalation is of major concern and can partly be explained by the long period of time taken in the design and construction of projects once the decision to proceed has been taken.

- All new transport infrastructure projects produce negative as well as positive externalities, which are invariably controversial (see also Chapter 2).

The Private Finance Initiative

The Private Finance Initiative (PFI) aims to identify projects which can attract private sector finance that can be used alongside public sector funding. The transport sector has been a leading area where this general principle has been applied and, as explained above, has been partly responsible for the surge in investment in transport over the past ten years or so.

Two main types of project have resulted. These are:

- Schemes largely funded by the private sector but with some investment by central and local government. Examples include the Channel Tunnel Rail Link, Cross Rail, Docklands Light Railway and new light rail systems such as the Croydon Tramlink, Midland Metro and Nottingham Express Transit.

- Schemes funded by the private sector but where the assets are transferred to the government when the project's concession ends. Examples include the second Severn Crossing, the Dartford Bridge, improvements to the West Coast main line and the M6 Toll Road (Birmingham Northern Relief Road).

On the surface the PFI appears to have much to commend it. The main advantage is that it is a way of increasing the amount of capital funding for transport projects, particularly when there are macroeconomic constraints on public expenditure growth. Given the escalating transport problems that the UK has to deal with, this has to be a major benefit. It is also a way of transferring risk to the private sector while using private sector expertise in the design, management and operation of a particular new project.

The PFI can, however, be criticised on three counts. Firstly, it can be argued that private funding is merely a substitute for public sector funding, with no overall gain in terms of increasing the scale of resources going into transport. Despite the actual increase in total investment, it could be argued that even more investment should be forthcoming from the public sector. Secondly, the private sector is looking for a good return on its investment – prices charged to users may therefore be higher than if the project had been built in the public sector and, in the case of roads, some might argue that use should be free of charge. A final criticism is that for most schemes, the public sector is required to underwrite the revenue that is generated by the project. Some would argue that because this reduces the risk to private investors, it is really no different to the public sector building a project using its own resources.

Cost-benefit analysis and its application in the provision of roads

In 2004/05, central and local government spent around £7800 million on the road network in the UK. Around 40 per cent of this total was expended on capital projects; the rest was mainly spent by local government on road maintenance and upkeep.

At first sight a road may seem to be a **public good**. This is a view that can be reinforced with the recognition that it would be very difficult for many roads to be provided by the private sector and that it makes little or no sense for there to be a duplication of resources. To be a pure public good, a road should have two characteristics, **non-excludability** and **non-rivalry**. Neither applies in full. For example:

- To demonstrate non-excludability, a road should be available to all. Nevertheless, there are other groups who are excluded, such as those too young or too old to drive. There are also 'free riders' in the case of roads. For example, overseas visitors and foreign hauliers use UK roads but do not necessarily contribute to the cost of their maintenance through taxation.
- To exhibit non-rivalry, the use of a stretch of road by one person must not prevent others from using it in the same way. Uncongested roads meet this requirement; roads that are heavily congested do not.

A road is best described as a **quasi-public good**, so called because some, but not all, of the characteristics of public goods are applicable.

Tackling the gridlock

In December 2002, the government announced a £5.5 billion package of widening motorways and some A roads alongside many local schemes to relieve some of the country's worst congestion problems (see Figure 1).

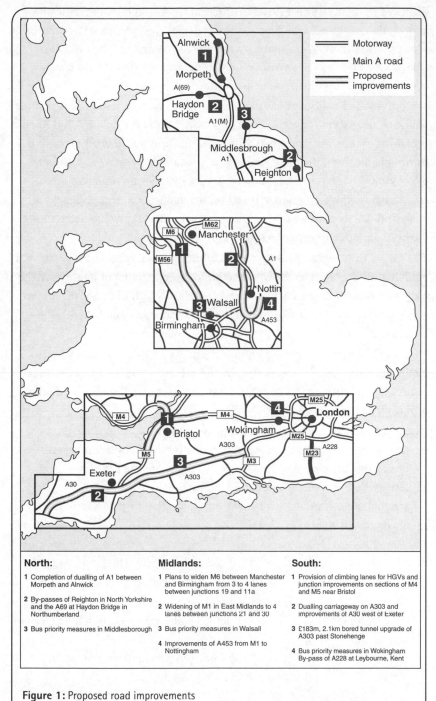

Figure 1: Proposed road improvements

North:

1 Completion of dualling of A1 between Morpeth and Alnwick

2 By-passes of Reighton in North Yorkshire and the A69 at Haydon Bridge in Northumberland

3 Bus priority measures in Middlesborough

Midlands:

1 Plans to widen M6 between Manchester and Birmingham from 3 to 4 lanes between junctions 19 and 11a

2 Widening of M1 in East Midlands to 4 lanes between junctions 21 and 30

3 Bus priority measures in Walsall

4 Improvements of A453 from M1 to Nottingham

South:

1 Provision of climbing lanes for HGVs and junction improvements on sections of M4 and M5 near Bristol

2 Dualling carriageway on A303 and improvements of A30 west of Exeter

3 £183m, 2.1km bored tunnel upgrade of A303 past Stonehenge

4 Bus priority measures in Wokingham By-pass of A228 at Leybourne, Kent

Critics of the plans warned that construction work would cause traffic chaos and would not solve the problems of congestion. The government's decision was, however, warmly welcomed by the director-general of the CBI who commented that: 'this is a sensible long-term package that should reduce congestion and sustain economic growth'.

The provision of roadspace has in modern times been the responsibility of the public sector, except for certain estuary crossings and the new M6 Toll Road for which charges are made. Use of the vast majority of the road network is free of charge. Until there is a national user charging system (see Chapter 5) certain criteria have to be followed in order to allocate resources in an effective way. These criteria are based on the application of **cost-benefit analysis** (CBA) and have particular significance when applied to determining the best allocation of capital resources.

CBA, as its name suggests, seeks to establish the social costs and benefits of a particular project such as the construction of a new stretch of motorway. The costs and benefits are estimated for the so-called length of life of the project – this can be 25–35 years. By looking at the social costs and benefits, the intention is to take as wide a view as the methodology permits.

In practice, the Department for Transport and its agencies use a computer model known as COBA to work out the **net present value** of any major road project that has been put forward for appraisal (see also *Cost-benefit analysis of rail projects* on page 43). The data input consists of:

- identification of the respective costs and benefits
- enumeration, or putting a monetary value on these costs and benefits
- forecasting the costs and benefits for each year of the life of a project
- discounting the annual costs and benefits
- arriving at a net present value, with an indication of the risks and uncertainties involved.

Figure 2 shows a simplified outline of the COBA model. The left hand side shows the two main costs of any road project. These are:

- capital costs that accrue in the early years of a major project and include the costs of land purchase, construction costs, design costs, administration and so on
- maintenance costs, which cover the projected annual costs of lighting, surface work, cleaning and routine maintenance.

The right hand side shows 'user costs'. At first sight this might be misleading since with any new road scheme, there are user cost savings compared to an otherwise 'do-minimum' approach. These savings are actually user benefits

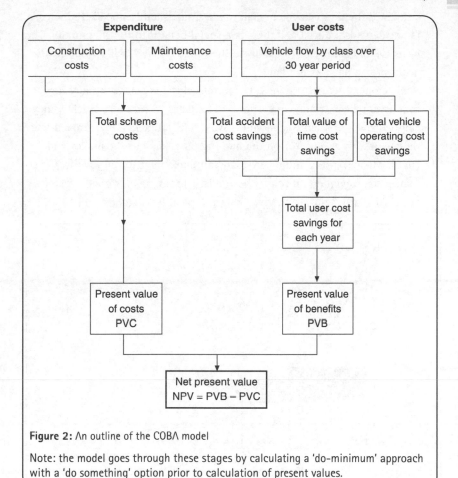

Figure 2: An outline of the COBA model

Note: the model goes through these stages by calculating a 'do-minimum' approach with a 'do something' option prior to calculation of present values.

since they represent a cost saving to those using the new road facility. More specifically, three user cost savings are shown. These are:

- Value of time cost savings. These are normally the most important benefit accruing to users of a new road. The rationale behind their inclusion is the opportunity cost of time spent in congested traffic. Typically, the regular car commuter spends around six days a year in queues of traffic; time that could be put to more productive use. If journey times can be reduced, the time saved can be used in a meaningful way for work or non-work purposes. (See *The valuation of time savings* on page 41, which explains how a value of time is estimated.)

- Accident cost savings. New motorways and by-passes are safer to travel on for their users than conventional roads. They also pose far less risk to pedestrians, particularly where a new by-pass replaces a road going straight through a village or small town. Consequently, the likely increase in accidents is reduced and there is a social benefit to the community. The basis for calculating this benefit can be found in *The costs of road traffic accidents* on page 21 in Chapter 2.

■ Vehicle operating cost savings. The point behind constructing any new road is to relieve traffic congestion. As vehicles travel more quickly, they can be driven in a more economical way. Fuel efficiency is improved and there is less wear and tear on the moving parts such as the brakes and clutch. Overall, users of the new road can make their journeys at less cost than when travelling on congested roads. The savings for goods vehicles are particularly significant, given that a typical large goods vehicle

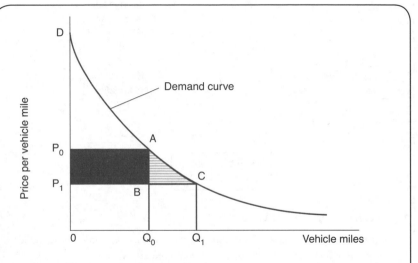

Assume that D is the market demand for travel. The effect of opening a new motorway is to reduce travel costs to users from P_0 to P_1 per vehicle mile. As with most demand curves, when the price falls more people will be willing to travel at a reduced price.

At this new reduced price, existing/former travellers will continue to travel. Their aggregate benefit is rectangle P_0ABP_1.

The reduced price also increases the demand for new users wishing to travel. This is known as the *benefit to generated traffic* and is shown by the 'triangle' ABC.

$$\text{Total traffic benefit} = P_0ABP_1 + ABC$$

Consumer surplus increases from DP_0A to DP_1C.

Figure 3: Benefits to users of a new motorway

consumes a litre of diesel for every kilometre travelled and that fuel costs amount to 35–40 per cent of total operating costs.

The valuation of time savings

Changes in travel time are major items in any cost-benefit analysis that is undertaken to secure government expenditure. The methodology involves putting a monetary value on the time savings depending on the journey purpose – work, commuting (to and from the normal place of work) and other (non-work) are the three categories that are distinguished. For each purpose, there is a further differentiation for the type of vehicle used, normally the car, goods vehicle and public service vehicle.

Travel in the course of work is valued the highest on the grounds that the value of the output produced in working time must be at least equal to the cost to the employer per hour of hiring labour for that time. This assumes all working time can be used to increase production. The value of time that is used is further increased to take into account employment charges.

The value of time spent commuting and for non-work purposes is more difficult to estimate since no direct market price is available. In these cases, an estimate is made from empirical studies of the trade offs between the speed and the cost that people are prepared to put up with for particular types of trip.

In all cases, travel time is costed on the same unit value – a saving of 30 minutes equates to the same as 30 savings of one minute each.

Based on 2002 values, a few typical values of time costs are shown below.

Table 2: Typical values of time costs

Type of vehicle	Pence per hour
Car	
– driver in course of work	2 186
– driver, commuting	417
– driver, non-work	368
Light goods vehicle	
– average	961
Public service vehicle	
– driver	842
– passenger, commuting	417
– passenger, other	368
Average value of time cost	900

Source: COBA Manual, Department for Transport, 2004

The COBA model has provided an appropriate basis for decisions to be taken on how to allocate capital resources for the UK's road network. It is a common model for all new road schemes and therefore assesses their need on a given basis. It is also a means of establishing need and how schemes can be ranked in order in terms of their net social benefit.

Notwithstanding this obvious need, in recent years there has been growing criticism of the COBA model on various grounds, including the following points:

- COBA is essentially a user-based method of appraisal. It estimates the monetary benefits to users of a new road in a consistent way but does not cover the full social benefits that might arise. In the case of a by-pass to a historic town, for example, there could be indirect or secondary effects in terms of reduced traffic noise, increased trade for retailers and a general improvement in amenities, particularly for those living on routes that have experienced traffic diversion.

- COBA does not include an estimate of the cost of negative externalities arising from the construction of a new road. Over the past 20 years or so, there has been increasing opposition to new road construction (the case of the Newbury by-pass for example) on environmental grounds. Protesters have objected to the impact in terms of loss of valuable land, loss of trees, damage to wildlife habitats, increased pollution and so on.

- Certain value judgements have to be made in order to estimate the user cost savings. These particularly concern the valuation of time and the costs of road accidents. As explained earlier, a shadow price has to be calculated as these variables cannot be estimated using market prices.

A 'new approach to appraisal'

In 1998, the government set out a new approach to the appraisal of trunk road schemes as part of its strategy for promoting integrated transport (see Chapter 6). This new approach is a wider ranging methodology which incorporates the COBA technique. It is based on five criteria, examples of which are shown in Table 3, in the context of the appraisal of new roads.

Although the new approach uses valuations from the COBA method, the underlying appraisal framework is not cost-benefit analysis. Additional information is provided on the impact of a road project on the community in the widest sense. Some of the valuations attempted, for example severance reduction, are particularly difficult to quantify. Also, unlike COBA, there is no attempt to reach a definite recommendation on the proposal by weighting the factors involved. Overall, though, the new approach is an improvement and step up from COBA in so far as it seeks to take into account some of the criticism that has been made in the past about the limitations of the COBA model.

Table 3: Criteria in the new appraisal methodology

Criterion	Variable	Valuation (£m)
Environmental impact	Air pollution	Air pollution reduction
	Noise pollution	Noise pollution reduction
	Greenhouse gas emissions	Change in emissions
	Landtake	–
Safety	Accident cost savings	as COBA
	Personal safety	Reduction in incidents
Economy	Journey time savings	as COBA
	Jobs created	–
Accessibility	Severance	Severance reduction
	Properties affected	Value of option
Integration	Contribution to improved modal Integration	–

Source: Department for Transport, 2001

Ideally, with an integrated transport policy, one technique should be used to determine public sector capital expenditure for all modes of transport. In this way, it would be possible to compare the case for a new road against that for, say, an upgrade on part of the rail network. While this integrated transport policy is much closer to being realised than it was a few years ago, it is, however, still some way off. Methodologically, there are many challenges for transport economists to overcome if an all-embracing approach is to receive the public acceptance that it needs if it is to be adopted.

Cost-benefit analysis of rail projects

In general, railways do not make money; they do though, provide wider social benefits. These are very important in the investment appraisal of capital projects for rail and in determining whether to continue to subsidise unremunerative passenger services. By using trains, people leave their cars at home and the roads are less congested. This represents an external benefit to the car drivers and to commercial vehicles that use the road network. This benefit can be quantified to justify capital and revenue support for railways. The external benefits can be extended to include environmental advantages of rail over road and the effects on the local economy.

Due to high capital costs, rail investment is long term in nature and often appraised over 30 years or more length of life. Figure 4 shows the basis of the appraisal. The stream of costs and benefits are estimated and then discounted to work out a present value; the outcome is a benefit cost ratio. A ratio greater than one means that for every pound invested, there is a financial and social benefit arising from the project. As a general rule, transport planners look for a ratio of 1.3:1 or better, largely to take into account the risks and uncertainties involved. Through this methodology, competing projects receive consistent and fair treatment.

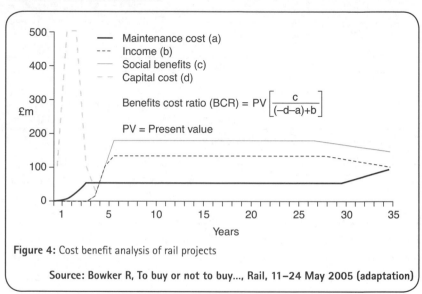

Figure 4: Cost benefit analysis of rail projects

Source: Bowker R, To buy or not to buy..., Rail, 11–24 May 2005 (adaptation)

Airport development in the UK

The demand for air travel by UK residents has increased five-fold in the last 30 years. In 2004, 216 million passengers passed through the UK's airports, with around one half of this total being UK residents making trips abroad. This represents a doubling in passenger volume since 1994. Moreover, air travel is predicted to grow by at least five per cent per annum over the next 25 years, resulting in an estimated 500 million passengers using our airports by 2030. Freight traffic has also experienced tremendous growth. In 2004, the UK's airports handled 2.4 million tonnes of freight, almost double the amount recorded in 1994.

Increasingly, due to the meteoric growth of low-fare carriers, much of this growth has been through less fashionable regional airports such as Luton, Liverpool, Bristol and Edinburgh. There are now around 80 no-frills airlines in Europe, with the UK being extensively served by the largest, Ryanair and easyJet. Notwithstanding, London's three main airports, Heathrow, Gatwick and Stansted, handle around 55 per cent of all passenger traffic. All have been owned since 1987 by the privatised British Airports Authority.

Airport development has caused major headaches for the government. The dilemma is that more capacity is needed in the South East, at Heathrow especially, yet from an environmental standpoint, any airport expansion is met by vehement complaints from environmental groups and people unfortunate enough to live under flight paths. A further complication is that the projected increases in passenger and freight traffic are in direct conflict with moves towards a more sustainable transport policy (see Chapter 6).

In December 2003, the government published a highly controversial white paper on the 'Future of Air Transport'. This document recognised the environmental problems and social costs of all air transport provision. It was also very clear on the need for various forms of indirect taxation to control or mitigate some of these effects (see Chapter 2). At the same time, it also recognised the obvious social benefits, as well as the need to meet the future rights and interests of those wanting to fly.

As well as tackling the taxation issue, two further key questions were evaluated. These were:

- Should new airport capacity be provided over the next 30 years, and if so, how much?
- Where should additional capacity be provided?

Ideally, the situation required a cost-benefit analysis to be carried out, which had been the response in 1969 with the Roskill Inquiry, although its recommendations were subsequently overruled. While the white paper raised many pertinent issues, it fell considerably short of being a cost-benefit analysis. Based on the previous strategy of safeguarding Heathrow's place as a major international hub, the government's new airport development strategy involved:

- no support for an alternative major new airport in the South East
- a second runway to be built at Stansted by 2012
- a third runway and sixth terminal for Heathrow by 2015–20, provided environmental problems regarding the flight path could be addressed. If not, Gatwick would have a new runway
- a second runway for Birmingham and extensions at other selected regional airports.

Figure 5 shows the full details.

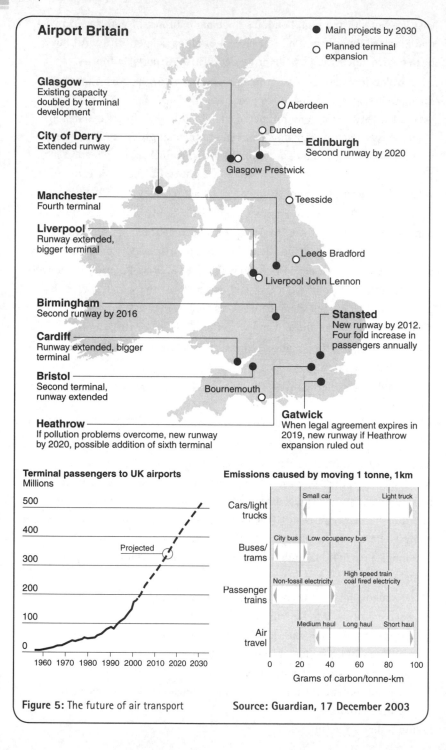

Airport Britain

● Main projects by 2030
○ Planned terminal expansion

Glasgow
Existing capacity doubled by terminal development

○ Aberdeen

○ Dundee

City of Derry
Extended runway

Edinburgh
Second runway by 2020

● ○
Glasgow Prestwick

Manchester
Fourth terminal

○ Teesside

Liverpool
Runway extended, bigger terminal

○ Leeds Bradford

○ Liverpool John Lennon

Birmingham
Second runway by 2016

Stansted
New runway by 2012. Four fold increase in passengers annually

Cardiff
Runway extended, bigger terminal

Bristol
Second terminal, runway extended

Bournemouth
○

Gatwick
When legal agreement expires in 2019, new runway if Heathrow expansion ruled out

Heathrow
If pollution problems overcome, new runway by 2020, possible addition of sixth terminal

Terminal passengers to UK airports
Millions

500

400

300 Projected

200

100

0

1960 1970 1980 1990 2000 2010 2020 2030

Emissions caused by moving 1 tonne, 1km

Cars/light trucks — Small car / Light truck

Buses/trams — City bus / Low occupancy bus

Passenger trains — Non-fossil electricity / High speed train coal fired electricity

Air travel — Medium haul / Long haul / Short haul

0   20   40   60   80   100
Grams of carbon/tonne-km

Figure 5: The future of air transport

Source: Guardian, 17 December 2003

This latest strategy document is broadly in line with previous discussions to continue to concentrate and expand airport provision in the South East. It does, however, differ from earlier policies through its related strategy on supporting the expansion of many regional airports, a clear recognition of the increasing role that is being played by low cost airlines in the market.

Airports are commercial organisations. The presumption is that the business case is fully supported by the British Airports Authority and others and that where applicable, planning permissions are given by their local authorities. In the case of Stansted especially, but also Heathrow, this is far from being automatic.

A commercial investment appraisal differs from CBA in various respects, for example:

- The wider social costs and benefits are not taken into account in the investment decision-making process.
- The income that is generated by airports from landing fees, retail outlets, peripheral services and so on has to be adequate to support the huge capital costs involved.
- Although overall traffic growth is reasonably secure, the attitude of the many airline operators to using a particular airport is subject to much greater risk and uncertainty – given their private ownership, the government is not allowed to offer subsidies.
- The rate of return on the capital investment is likely to be higher than that for a publicly-funded development.
- There is further uncertainty over the measures that might be used by the government to reduce market failures associated with further airport development.

Summary

On completion of this chapter you have learnt that:

- as capital resources for transport investment are limited relative to wants, some means of resource allocation is required
- most investment in transport is carried out by the public sector; for air transport and increasingly for rail and road, the private sector is taking a growing interest
- cost-benefit analysis is a reasonably effective way of allowing resource allocation decisions to be made by the public sector, although recently, a new, wider approach to transport investment appraisal has been used
- the case of airport investment provides an interesting example of the private and public sectors making decisions on transport investment.

Useful websites

Department for Transport www.dft.gov.uk (click on economics and appraisal)

Activities

Topics for investigation

Look back over the past 10 years or so of data on investment in transport (see www.dft.gov.uk/transportstatistics). What evidence is there to link general changes in transport investment over this period to changes in transport policy?

Exam-style practice questions

Data response questions

1. Study Figure 4 on page 44 on the costs and benefits of a rail project. At a 10 per cent discount rate, this produces a benefit cost ratio of 1.62:1. What does this mean? (5)

2. Suppose there are two competing projects, both with a benefit cost ratio of 1.62. The first is like that shown in the diagram. The second has a small capital cost, less receipts and will be spread over a much shorter period. Discuss which project you would recommend to proceed. (10)

Essay questions

1. Explain the private and external costs arising from the construction of new trunk roads and motorways. (10)

2. Discuss whether estimates for such costs alone are sufficient in decision-making regarding the construction of new trunk roads, by-passes and motorways. (15)

    (OCR, Module 2885, January 2004)

3. Explain the difference between a cost-benefit and commercial appraisal for a new airport development. Comment upon the circumstances when both might be appropriate. (25)

4 Market structures and competitive behaviour in transport markets

In this chapter, you will learn:

- what is meant by a transport market
- how the models of market structure can be applied to selected transport markets
- why barriers to entry are very important in determining the degree of competition in transport markets
- what is meant by a contestable market
- how deregulation has sought to produce competitive markets for local bus services in Britain and for European air transport services
- the arguments for and against the privatisation of transport
- how railways in Britain have been privatised
- how the effectiveness of rail privatisation can be evaluated.

Key words contestable market • contestability • cross-subsidisation
deregulation • dominant monopoly • economies of scale
efficiency • flexible pricing • franchising • intimidation
limit pricing • local monopoly • logistics • market structure
monopolistic competition • monopoly • natural monopoly
oligopoly • perfect competition • price discrimination
predatory pricing • premium payment • privatisation
productive efficiency • regulatory barriers • set up costs
sub-market • sunk costs

Transport markets

Unlike product markets, it is not always easy to define a market in the service sector. This is particularly the case with transport markets, as explained in the definition of transport in Chapter 1. A transport market consists of buyers and sellers of transport services like any other market; it is best analysed as a collection of **sub-markets**. This is shown in Figure 1.

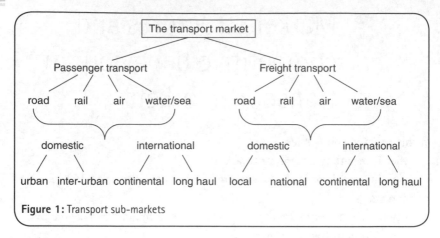

Figure 1: Transport sub-markets

As this figure indicates, there is a basic distinction between passenger transport and freight transport. For each, the main modes of transport can be applied; in turn, sub-markets based on the length of haul or journey can be incorporated. From a business perspective, firms might operate in one or more of these defined sub-markets. It is therefore important from an applied standpoint to be aware of the particular sub-market or sub-markets in which firms operate.

Market structures

The term **market structure** is used in Economics to describe the way in which a market is organised in terms of how many firms there are, how they vary in size and whether firms produce goods or services that are close substitutes for each other. For many years, economists have recognised four main market structures. These are **perfect competition, monopolistic competition, oligopoly and monopoly.** Their relative characteristics are analysed in all standard introductory text books (for example, see Grant S and Vidler C, *Economics AS and A2 for OCR* and Griffiths A and Ison S, *Business Economics*, Heinemann, 2001). To set the context for this chapter, a summary of these characteristics is given in Table 1.

In transport markets, the degree of competition tends to be determined by two of the characteristics shown in Table 1. These are:

■ Barriers to entry. The extent to which it is possible for new firms to enter a market. These tend to be varied and often substantial, meaning that transport markets are often not as competitive as they might seem to be. Barriers to entry become more effective in oligopoly and monopoly than in the other two market structures given in Table 1.

Table1: Principal market structures

	Perfect competition	Monopolistic competition	Oligopoly	Monopoly
Number of firms	Many	Many	Dominated by a few	One
Size of firms	Very small	Small	Large	Variable
Barriers to entry	None	Few	High	Very high
Type of product	The same or homogeneous	Differentiated	Varied e.g. branding	No close substitutes
Firm's influence on price	Price takers	Price makers	Price makers	Price makers
	Benchmark by which other market structures can be evaluated from an efficiency standpoint	Normal profits only in long run. Firms are not allocatively or productively efficient	Firms are often interdependent. Occasional price wars. Heavy non-price competition	Often now seen as a firm with a 25% market share. 40% market share = dominant monopoly

- The number of firms. In contrast, the two competitive market structures are characterised by large numbers of invariably small firms. This is conducive to competition and an efficient allocation of resources. So, as the number of firms in a market increases, so does the competition between them. Conversely, fewer firms usually means that there is very little competition in the market.

Over the years, as transport markets have grown in size, the barriers to entry have become more of an obstacle for new firms wishing to enter a particular market. These include:

- High **set up costs**. Although firms often lease expensive transport vehicles, the cost of entry into the rail passenger and air transport markets is formidable and can run into many millions of pounds. A fleet of vehicles is invariably needed if a new firm is going to make any impact when in competition against established operators.

- **Sunk costs.** These are costs that cannot be recovered if a firm ceases to operate in a market and can also be very high. Again, such costs act as a deterrent to entry in transport markets where future profitability is uncertain.

- **Regulatory barriers.** The licensing of all types of transport vehicle and their drivers has been a traditional way of trying to achieve quality in transport markets. In addition, where passengers are carried, health and safety and public liability regulations have to be adhered to. It is also the case in the EU that all businesses, irrespective of their size, cannot legally provide transport services without an Operator's Licence.

- **Economies of scale.** Established firms, particularly monopolies, may benefit from various types of economies of scale and produce close to their minimum efficient scale of operations. As a consequence, the average long run costs of established firms are usually less that those of prospective new entrants. Economies of scale are important in almost any transport market where large, powerful firms have a strong market presence. A particularly good example is that of low-fare airlines. By using their aeroplanes very intensively, the average cost per passenger can be reduced to a very competitive level compared to other operators who might not be using their planes as efficiently.

- **Limit pricing.** Through pricing below average cost, an established firm is able to prevent new firms from entering a market. This tactic has been used in some local bus markets following **deregulation** and has prompted investigation by the Competition Commission (formerly the Monopolies and Mergers Commission). This is good for consumers in the short run, but invariably bad in the long run where a monopoly or near-monopoly might increase its prices.

- **Intimidation.** This is not unknown although it is very difficult to prove. Established companies can use threats and other tactics to keep out any would-be new entrants to their markets. It has reputedly been applied by large established operators in local bus markets.

- **Franchising.** Through a franchise, a firm may be given, often after competitive bidding, the exclusive right to provide a particular service to the exclusion of others. This right would normally be given by a body that has responsibility for transport provision such as the former Strategic Rail Authority, or the Transport for London organisation in the case of bus routes in the capital.

With respect to the number of firms, the extent of competition in transport markets is not as clear as in the case of barriers to entry. One important reason for this is the extent to which there is **contestability** in the market (see *Contestable markets* on page 53). As stated earlier, transport markets with a large number of firms are likely to be more competitive that those with just one or a handful of firms.

It is increasingly common for transport markets to contain fewer and fewer firms. This is one of the outcomes of deregulation, the removal of barriers to entry into a market, although it was not the intention when deregulation was suggested by policy makers. At the time, it was believed that deregulation would increase competition and produce a situation where many small firms would be competing in local markets. The reality is that mergers and takeovers have reduced competition. Depending on how the market is defined, some transport markets are a monopoly because there is just one company providing services. Most markets though, are dominated by a relatively small number of firms and display all the signs of being an oligopolistic market.

Of the two determining factors, the strength of the barriers to entry more so than the number of firms, is most likely to determine the extent to which a particular transport market is competitive. Although it is by no means straightforward, there is some relationship between these determinants and the extent of competition. This is shown in Figure 2.

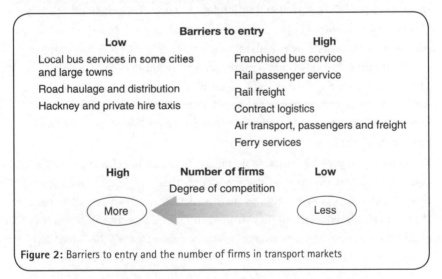

Figure 2: Barriers to entry and the number of firms in transport markets

Contestable markets

A **contestable market** is a situation where there is free entry into a market and exit from the market is costless. Conceptually, the idea was developed by the American economist William Baumol in the mid-1970s and subsequently applied to the deregulation of US domestic air transport services. The principle has underpinned much of UK transport policy over the past 25 years or so.

A perfectly contestable market exists where the threat of a new firm entering a market forces the incumbent firm or firms to behave as though this threat was being realised. In principle, there should be a pool of new potential entrants behaving in this way. This means:

- new firms will enter the market if excessive profits are being earned
- in the long run, profits will return to normal as a consequence of the 'hit and run' tactics of these new firms who are happy to take short term gains
- the operating costs of new firms should be the same as those of firms already operating in the markets
- the number and size of firms is irrelevant and will be determined by the market
- the nature of the product can be varied.

Aside from the principles, it is necessary for regulatory bodies (e.g. the Office of Fair Trading and the Competition Commission) to be in a position to ensure fair play. In particular, their role is to monitor the behaviour of firms in terms of **predatory pricing** and intimidation, both of which could severely reduce competition.

Although economists now talk about contestable markets, it is important to bear in mind that this is not a market structure alongside those set out in Table 1. In some ways it is less confusing to refer to contestability in a market since the condition can apply to any market structure, monopoly and oligopoly included, as long as the essential pre-requisites of free entry and costless exit apply.

The beauty of a perfectly contestable market is that it matches a perfectly competitive market as far as **efficiency** is concerned. All firms should therefore charge a price equal to average – usually long run average – cost. If price is above average cost, new firms will enter due to the attraction of excess profits. Any firm that charges below average cost will be forced out of the market. This is the condition for **productive efficiency**, whereby all firms operate at minimum average cost. Firms should also charge a price that equals marginal cost. By doing this, the problem of **cross-subsidisation** is avoided and the conditions for **allocative efficiency** are being met. A perfectly competitive market produces a situation in which allocative and productive efficiency are achieved. The three other market structures are imperfectly competitive and do not achieve either type of efficiency. The objective of contestability is to create as far as possible the conditions of a perfectly competitive market in any such market structure.

A perfectly contestable market also provides benefits for consumers. As the price paid is equal to average cost and in turn, marginal cost, there is less likelihood of consumers being exploited. This is further clear reasoning as to why those responsible for determining transport policies should aim to realise contestability in all types of transport markets.

Deregulation

The aim of deregulation is to remove or relax government rules and regulations controlling the operation of firms in a particular activity. Deregulation therefore facilitates contestability, usually in markets that have traditionally had substantial regulation and little or no competition.

This is particularly true of transport markets where barriers to entry protected public sector monopoly operators from competition. Between the mid-1980s and the late-1990s, domestic bus and air transport markets were deregulated and European road freight and air markets liberalised to produce a much more competitive environment.

Deregulation – local bus services in Britain

It is now over 20 years since the Transport Act of 1985 established a supposedly contestable market in the local bus industry. The only barrier to entry was that all firms needed an Operator's Licence, largely for safety reasons in order to ensure minimum quality standards. Firms were also required to register services with the regional Traffic Commissioners and to notify them when services were added, withdrawn or amended. Significantly, companies were free to charge whatever fares they thought the market would bear. Local authorities and, in the conurbations, the Passenger Transport Executives, were given the responsibility for funding socially necessary services, normally through a tendering process. The outcome is that local bus services are in two distinct types, those that are commercial and those that require external support.

At the time of deregulation, there was considerable opposition to the former Conservative government's plans from the trade unions, the public sector companies themselves and from local and national politicians. This opposition was based on fear of the unknown, in so far as nowhere else in the world had sought to create a contestable market on the scale covered by the 1985 legislation.

Deregulation was accompanied by a long, drawn out and in many respects, messy programme of **privatisation**. Through this, the former National Bus Company subsidiaries (65 in all) were soon disposed of, followed by Passenger

Transport Executive (PTE) and some local authority owned operations. Some of the latter remain in a form of public ownership under the control of unitary authorities in towns such as Blackburn, Blackpool, Ipswich, Nottingham and Plymouth. They are though, required to operate on a full commercial basis.

The local bus industry is, therefore, almost entirely privately owned and has been for some time, with firms competing in a contestable market. The notable exception is in London, where the proposed deregulation was hastily aborted in 1993 in favour of retaining a franchise system that had been very effective since 1984. Through this system, companies bid for the right to run a particular service or network of services subject to certain conditions relating to route frequency and significantly, fare levels and the acceptance of Oyster and the London Travelcard. Unlike the rest of Great Britain, there is no competition and no opportunity for contestability to influence the allocation of resources.

At the time, deregulation was seen as the last chance to save an industry in apparent terminal decline. Politically, it was viewed as a way of letting the private sector correct the many perceived weaknesses of public ownership and of a heavily regulated market. As the first country to attempt this aspect of deregulation on a large scale, there was no precedent. It was firmly believed that there was an opportunity for small local firms to enter the market and remain there as contestable market principles might indicate.

The effects of this deregulation are not easy to generalise, although the following points have been identified in various empirical studies:

- The degree of competition in the market varies from city to city, town to town. It is though, quite limited in many respects as the major groups now have a considerable share of the overall market (see Figure 3). Some groups also hold rail franchises and in some cases, operate light rail systems and have overseas interests. They have emerged as powerful businesses as a consequence of deregulation. Although difficult to prove, they seem reluctant to compete head on with each other, and in many cases have technical **local monopolies**.
- Smaller companies continue to exist but largely at the margin, invariably providing services in relation to localised need.
- Many urban services, especially on corridors into large towns and cities, are now of greater frequency than at the time of deregulation.
- Fare levels in most places have continued to rise above the rate of inflation. Some fare competition exists, for example smaller companies with older vehicles undercutting the major groups.
- Service instability remains a major issue, with route changes and timetables altering with monotonous regularity.

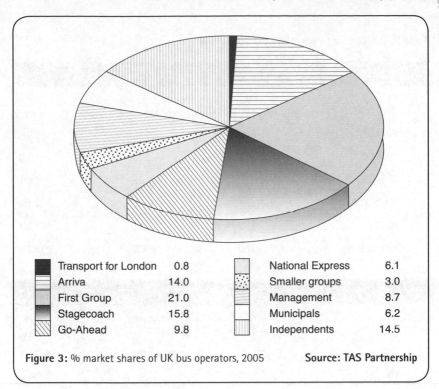

■	Transport for London	0.8	National Express	6.1
	Arriva	14.0	Smaller groups	3.0
	First Group	21.0	Management	8.7
	Stagecoach	15.8	Municipals	6.2
	Go-Ahead	9.8	Independents	14.5

Figure 3: % market shares of UK bus operators, 2005   **Source: TAS Partnership**

- Cross-subsidisation has not entirely been removed and tends to occur where the continuation of uneconomic services contributes to the overall revenue and profitability of a business.
- London excepted, external public subsidy has been reduced. In some areas this has allowed PTEs and local authorities to divert the savings to support local rail networks.

To the economist, various **efficiency** issues can be raised, for example:

- Has deregulation provided an improvement in allocative efficiency?
- Is there any evidence that productive efficiency has increased?

The information in Table 2 can be used to investigate these issues, albeit in a crude way. (See the data response question at the end of this chapter.) The following conclusions can be drawn:

- The near removal of cross-subsidisation has brought fare levels more in line with marginal costs.

Table 2: Bus market trends, 1994/95–2004/05

England outside London		
	Passenger journeys (m)	Operating costs per vehicle km[1, 2]	Fare index[3]
1994/95	2 603	103	96.8
1996/97	2 506	96	106.6
1998/99	2 436	97	118.2
2000/01	2 414	99	129.2
2002/03	2 355	97	140.8
2004/05	2 250	103	152.5

London		
	Passenger journeys (m)	Operating costs per vehicle km[1]	Fare index[3]
1994/95	1 155	190	96.2
1996/97	1 230	188	105.4
1998/99	1 266	178	113.7
2000/01	1 347	184	117.2
2002/03	1 527	215	114.8
2004/05	1 782	220	126.8

Note: [1] At 2004/05 prices.
        [2] Refers to Great Britain outside London.
        [3] 1995 = 100. Statistics for Great Britain outside London.

Source: Public Transport Statistics Bulletin GB, 2005 edition, Department for Transport

- Outside London, operating costs per vehicle kilometre have been falling until 2004/05 when escalating fuel prices caused a steep rise.
- Where there is local competition consumers may benefit in the short run especially.

The view of free market economists is that the flow of benefits following deregulation outside London has been considerable. They also claim that these benefits have been denied to operators in London since the terms of their franchises do not allow them discretion in seeking to mix price and quality in order to maximise consumer satisfaction. In short, they believe that deregulation works.

In other respects, deregulation has not been anywhere near as effective as was expected. The decline in the number of passenger journeys outside London has persisted. This has been greatest in the former English PTE areas – from 1994/95 to 2004/05, there was an 18.6 per cent decline. Fare levels in the same period have risen around 25 per cent in real terms. The market also tends to be dominated by the major groups, raising serious doubts about the extent to which this particular market really is contestable.

European logistics providers – an emerging oligopoly

Logistics is the term used to describe the ways in which businesses manage their supply chains. It covers all aspects, including the sourcing of goods and

Table 3: Total logistics revenues € million and growth (%), 2004

	Company	€m	Growth %
Tier one	Exel	8 960.8	25.2
	Schenker	8 042.0	17.3
	NYK Logistics	7 975.8	7.0
	Kuehne & Nagel	7 431.6	21.2
	DPWN	6 786.0	15.4
Tier two	Logista	4 406.4	8.0
	TNT Logistics	4 081.7	9.3
	Panalpina	3 964.8	14.1
	Ryder	3 775.9	7.2
	Geodis	3 370.6	4.8
Tier three	Gefco	2 894.0	5.5
	Wincanton	2 437.9	2.7
	Dachser	2 400.0	14.3
	ABX LOGISTICS	2 366.0	2.5
	Hellmann Worldwide Logistics	2 018.7	0.1
	SDV	1 943.0	7.3
	Thiel Logistik	1 730.4	10.3
	UPS SCS	1 719.9	4.0
	STEF–TFE	1 401.3	4.0
	Norbert Dentressangle	1 303.0	6.6
	ACR LOGISTICS	1 300.0	–
	Christian Salvesen	1 123.3	-4.1
	Frans Maas	1 091.4	6.9
	TDG	724.2	-5.2
	Gist	414.2	0.5

Source: Analytiqa. Note: Excluding CAT and Maersk Logistic

raw materials, their collection and storage and final sale to consumers. As an area of management it is now recognised to be of fundamental importance in the overall competitiveness of a company or organisation.

Increasingly, the logistics function has been contracted out by manufacturers, retailers and others to specialist companies such as those shown in Table 3. At the same time, the completion of the Single European Market and the 2004 geographical enlargement of the EU have provided new market opportunities. The UK's Exel has experienced considerable growth and is now the largest logistics company in Europe. Its growth has been helped enormously through its merger with the Ocean Group in 2001 and its acquisition of Tibbett and Britten in 2004. In September 2005, Exel itself was taken over by Deutsche Post World Net (DPWN), the world's largest mail, express delivery and logistics organisation. The industry is highly competitive, with low margins. It continues to be shaped by consolidation such as those changes involving Exel, yet overall, the industry remains fragmented with literally hundreds of other smaller companies providing various forms of logistics services.

Deregulation – European air services

The market for air transport in the EU has been deregulated since April 1997 when member states finally agreed to remove cabotage restrictions. Prior to this, the market had been heavily regulated, mainly in the form of bilateral agreements between member states. These clearly favoured national airlines such as British Airways and Lufthansa and state-owned national airlines such as Air France and Alitalia. In principle, the market is now contestable.

The effects of this deregulation have been substantial. These include:

- New entrants into the market, especially low-fare airlines. This is consistent with contestability and has undoubtedly been the most spectacular consequence of deregulation. Within the UK, Ryanair, easyJet, flybe and bmibaby are now well established and have expanded their businesses in spectacular fashion, although there have also been casualties, notably Go and Buzz, low-fare subsidiaries of British Airways and KLM respectively. In all, there are now around 70 low-fare European airlines.
- New routes, particularly those set up by low-fare airlines from smaller regional airports such as Luton (easyJet), Leeds Bradford (Jet 2) as well as Stansted (Ryanair), to usually smaller airports in the rest of the EU. These routes have been extended into the new applicant countries since May 2004.
- **Flexible pricing** based on yield management, the aim of which is to maximise revenue from each flight. Seat availability and prices are

monitored on a daily basis, with most passengers booking online through the internet. Flights are available on a single basis, often at ludicrously low fares or even zero fare, with customers just paying the taxes. Those booking later tend to pay premium fares. Over-booking is typical, the airlines assuming that some passengers who have paid the lowest fares may not turn up for travel.

- 'No frills' service, with strict check-in and baggage handling windows, no food or drink included in the fare and usually, no seat reservations. Airport turnaround costs tend to be around half those of scheduled carriers.

These effects, coupled with a range of external factors, have placed pressure on established national airlines in recent years. Some, such as Sabena (Belgium) and Swissair, have folded – the aftermath of 9/11/2001 was the last straw for them trying to compete in an already difficult trading market.

A second response has been for airlines to merge. The best example of this was the 2003 merger between Air France and KLM that was designed to return these businesses to profitability through cutting costs while improving the frequency and quality of services available through the partnership.

A third response has been for more airlines to join one of the three world-wide alliances. Major European airlines are members of each of the three main alliances, Oneworld (BA), Star Alliance (Lufthansa) and Skyteam (Air France, Alitalia). The purpose of alliances is to offer 'code share' services in order to reduce total costs and provide a 'hub and spoke' network of services: from regional/national spokes to a central hub. Short turnarounds, integrated baggage handling and check-in priority enhance the quality of the travel experience.

The European air passenger market is contestable but only to a limited extent. The national airlines occupy most of the take-off and landing slots at principal airports such as Heathrow. This represents a substantial barrier to entry. Alliances are anti-competitive and seek to protect the interests of their members as well as provide an attractive network of services for customers. Safety compliance and financial guarantee requirements also serve as barriers to entry to small, new operators. Yet despite these barriers, the growth of low-fare airlines has continued and the signs are that this growth will be maintained in the future.

Case study: Ryanair soars past BA

British Airways, which for years thrived on trumpeting itself as 'the world's favourite airline', has been hit by perhaps the ultimate ignominy – being overtaken in size by the upstart Irish budget airline Ryanair.

Today, for the first time in the brave new world of budget airlines, Ryanair, which only flies in Europe, said it carried more passengers in one month than the whole of BA.

Stricken by the damaging Gate Gourmet catering strike and bedevilled by tough competition, BA today reported it carried 127 000 fewer passengers in August than in the same month a year ago. At 3.101 million passengers that represents a fall of nearly four per cent.

Perhaps more damaging for BA, however, was the news that latest monthly figures out from Ryanair show that, in August, BA carried 156 000 fewer passengers than the Irish airline which saw numbers soar by 37 per cent to 3.257 million.

Michael O'Leary, the outspoken chief executive of Ryanair, was jubilant. 'It's official. Ryanair has today become the world's favourite airline. Last month, Ryanair's traffic exceeded BA's worldwide passengers across its entire network.'

O'Leary said BA's passenger fall was not just because of strikes but because of the fuel surcharges the flag-carrier has slapped on its ticket prices.

'Ryanair's passenger volumes are growing rapidly thanks to Ryanair's guarantee of no fuel surcharges – not today, not tomorrow, not ever,' he said.

'At least on Ryanair, customers can buy a sandwich with the £100 they have saved over BA's high fares and that's why BA are now officially just second choice.'

Ryanair has been carrying more passengers than BA in the short haul market for some time: today's figure reveals the Irish airline carried 1.1 million, or nearly 40 per cent more, passengers in Europe and the UK last month.

Source: Evening Standard, 5 September 2005

Privatisation of the transport industry in the UK

In a simple sense, privatisation refers to a change in ownership from the public sector to the private sector. During the 1980s transport, along with fuel, power and telecommunications, was subject to a massive and radical change from being a heavily regulated public sector activity to one that was largely deregulated and in the hands of the private sector. Over a short period of time, publicly owned freight services, bus services, ferry services, airports and the national airline were systematically sold off to new private owners. The largest sales took the form of a public floatation; smaller businesses were sold off and in some cases, were the subject of management buyouts.

The general case for privatisation applies to the transport industry. Four main benefits can be recognised:

- Privatisation provides a series of supply side-benefits for consumers due to an activity being exposed to the free market. Costs are reduced and greater productive efficiency is achieved as businesses respond to the needs of the market.
- Wider share ownership. This was an important political objective to involve all workers in the future well-being of a business.
- A reduction in public sector borrowing due to receipts from the sale of state-owned assets being used to fund current government expenditure.
- An opportunity for managers to have the freedom to manage without restrictive controls being imposed on them by the government.

On the other hand, particularly in the case of transport, counter privatisation arguments apply. For instance:

- Transport is a vitally important sector of the economy, essential for private and business well-being. Therefore, it can be argued that it should not be in the hands of the private sector for strategic reasons and for broader reasons of public interest. Under certain circumstances, cross-subsidisation would be acceptable, for example where rural bus and rail services are supported by revenue from more profitable urban services.
- Certain types of transport activity produce external benefits and should therefore be kept in the hands of the public sector. Rail is a particularly good example whereby external benefits are created through an efficient railway network reducing road congestion, accidents and atmospheric pollution.
- The **natural monopoly** argument. This is particularly relevant in the case of railways (see below). If unregulated, a natural monopoly could charge higher prices and produce a less efficient allocation of resources when in the private sector.
- The short term benefits of privatisation. Where an activity has been sold off, its financial benefit is short term in so far as the funds raised from the sale tend to be put to immediate use. Once committed, no further resources will be available.

Rail privatisation in Britain

Britain has had a privatised railway since 1994 when the first passenger franchises were awarded to private sector train operating companies. Of all the transport privatisations, this was at the time, and in some respects still is, the most controversial. Critics, including Mrs Thatcher, believed that this was 'a privatisation too far' for various reasons, including:

■ The practical problems of privatising a transport activity which had its own infrastructure and where safety had to be an overriding consideration ahead of commercial pressures.

■ The former British Rail was a loss-making business that required substantial subsidy from central and local government for its continuation.

■ No other country had attempted to privatise its railways on the scale put forward for Britain.

■ The natural monopoly argument. This recognises that the very nature of railway operations means that economies of scale continue to accrue to customers even where there is a dominant producer. It is also recognised that the duplication of services in this market structure represent a waste of resources.

Figure 4 shows the basis of the natural monopoly argument, linked to the

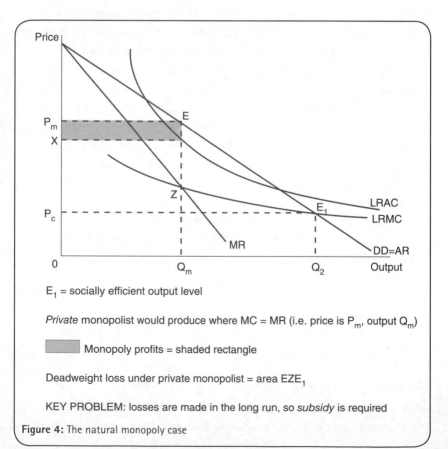

E_1 = socially efficient output level

Private monopolist would produce where MC = MR (i.e. price is P_m, output Q_m)

Monopoly profits = shaded rectangle

Deadweight loss under private monopolist = area EZE_1

KEY PROBLEM: losses are made in the long run, so *subsidy* is required

Figure 4: The natural monopoly case

on-going need for subsidy. This has particular relevance for railway operation where capital costs are high. Economies of scale accrue as shown by the LRAC curve not having reached its minimum point. The LRMC curve is below it, indicating that the monopolist can continue to gain from economies of scale as the level of output increases.

The dilemma for a natural monopoly is that it cannot survive as a profit maximising business, producing at output Q_m, while it continues to produce at the social optimum of P_cQ_2. Consequently, subsidy is required to support the monopolist to operate at this point. Historically this has been a powerful argument in support of state ownership of an activity such as railways.

Notwithstanding all of these issues, the 'New Opportunities for British Rail' White paper of 1992 put forward some powerful economic arguments for privatisation. These included:

- to see better use of the railways
- to provide greater responsiveness to the customer
- to see a higher quality service
- to give better value for money for rail users
- to generate new capital investment.

Moreover, there was a very blunt statement that 'public sector ownership is seen as a genuine obstacle towards achieving the above objectives...radical change is needed'. Privatisation was therefore seen as the only way forward. The approach that has been taken consists of:

- The separation of the infrastructure, for example, track and signalling, from passenger and freight train operations. This model, first proposed by the Adam Smith Institute, was eventually chosen after intense controversy about how this complex privatisation should take place. Alternative models that were evaluated were for the operations and track to be franchised to a small number of regional companies or for a broader sector privatisation based on the main business segments of the former British Rail.
- Passenger services to be franchised as service groups to train operating companies. In total 23 franchises are now available, with decisions on who operates what being taken by the Department for Transport (see Table 4). The majority of franchises carry a subsidy from central government; a small number including those operated by GNER, Thameslink and One Railway require the train operator to make an annual **premium payment** to run services. Net payments to train operating companies were around £1000 million in 2004/05.

- Freight services operating on a commercial full costs basis. Freight operators are required to pay commercial track charges, as well as having responsibility for paying for their use of rolling stock (see Table 5).
- Infrastructure to be owned and managed by a single organisation. This is now Network Rail which can be described as a not-for-profit company. Although publicly funded, it is a private organisation and is required to operate commercially. It replaced Railtrack, a private company with shareholders, following Railtrack's bankruptcy in 2002. Network Rail is also responsible for contracting out maintenance to various service companies.

The whole complex operation and behaviour of companies is overseen by a regulator, the Office of Rail Regulation. This body sets out minimum service levels and can impose heavy fines on train operating companies that fail to achieve required standards.

Table 4: Train operating companies in 2005

Franchisee	Franchise operator	
National Express Group	c2c Central Trains Gatwick Express Midland Mainline	Silverlink WAGN Wessex Trains
First Group plc (and subsidiaries)	First Great Western First Great Western Link	First ScotRail Transpennine Express
Stagecoach Group	Island Line	South West Trains
Go-Ahead Group	Southern	Thameslink
Virgin Rail Group	Virgin Cross Country	Virgin West Coast
Arriva Trains Ltd	Arriva Trains Wales	
M40 Trains Ltd	Chiltern Railways	
GNER Holdings Ltd	GNER	
Northern Rail Ltd	Northern Rail	
London Eastern Railway	One Railway	
South Eastern Trains Ltd	South Eastern Trains	

Other non-franchise operators are Merseyrail, Heathrow Express, Hull Trains, Stansted Express and Eurostar (UK).

Source: Strategic Rail Authority

A major structural change came in July 2004 with the decision to wind up the Strategic Rail Authority. This body had been responsible for promoting rail use and for strategically developing the rail network. It had also managed the award of franchises to train operating companies (see above). The consequence of this change is that the government, through the Department for Transport, is now in firm control. This has in general been welcomed, given the huge importance of rail in future transport policy (see chapter 6).

Table 5: Freight Operating Companies

Freight operator	
English, Welsh and Scottish Railway (EWS)	The largest operator with around 80 per cent of the total freight market. Much of its business is in the traditional market of moving heavy commodities such as coal, aggregates and petrochemicals. Aggressive marketing has seen it move into new food and drink, and retail goods markets.
Freightliner	Its core business is the movement of road-rail intermodal containers within the UK, particularly between inland terminals and container ports. The company is now competing in some markets with EWS.
Direct Rail Services (DRS)	A specialist company that carries nuclear materials for BNFL. Now moving into the general freight sector, with intermodal logistics provision.
GB Railfreight	Operates engineering trains for Network Rail and has developed new intermodal services from Felixstowe to inland terminals.

Source: Strategic Rail Authority

One of the objectives of rail privatisation was to increase the level of competition in the industry. This has happened but in only a limited way. For example:

- Rail passenger franchise operators are afforded some protection from 'open access' operators that seek to compete against them in particular markets. New franchises are given two years to establish themselves before direct competitors are allowed to set up rival services. They are also protected if it is felt that a new operator entering the market would lead to excess capacity on a route. This happened when Virgin Cross Country introduced increased services along the East Coast main line to Edinburgh and were forced to cut back frequencies after GNER complained to the Strategic Rail Authority.
- One of the few new operators to enter the market has been Hull Trains, which runs a limited service between Humberside and London Kings Cross

in competition with GNER. Another form of competition is where there is a geographical overlap of routes such as between Peterborough and London (GNER and WAGN) or between Birmingham and London (Virgin Trains, Chiltern Railways and Silverlink).

■ More examples of competition can be found in the rail freight sector, where there are no explicit barriers to entry to new firms. In principle, any new firm can enter this market, although in practice, the high set up costs deter would-be entrants. As Tables 4 and 5 indicate, there is competition between the main providers of domestic and international rail and intermodal services. This market, unlike rail passenger transport, is technically contestable.

Has rail privatisation succeeded?

This is not an easy question to answer as there have been some successes and winners but also some failures and losers. Table 6 shows, in crude terms using a base year of 1995, some key measures of performance for the privatised railway system. It shows very clearly that:

■ The volume of rail passenger travel has increased by around one third following privatisation. This is a clear reversal of a trend of long term decline over the 35 years prior to privatisation.

■ The increase in the use of rail to transport freight has been even greater, again reversing a trend of long term decline, this time over an even longer period.

■ Investment in infrastructure and new rolling stock has increased spectacularly. Much of the latter has been sourced from the privatised train operating and rolling stock companies. The consequence has been a clearly visible and much needed upgrading in the quality of railway rolling stock.

■ An increase in levels of subsidy paid by central and local government to the train operating companies, from 2001–02 especially.

Even at this crude level, it is evident that some of the objectives of privatisation that were spelled out in the 'New Opportunities' white paper and subsequent Railways Act have been achieved.

One of the reasons for the increase in passenger journeys has been the way in which many of the mainline train operating companies have been able to exploit their monopoly power through **price discrimination**. Leisure travellers have been the main beneficiaries, provided they are flexible in their travel plans.

Table 6: Key performance indicators following privatisation

	1995	2004	% change
Passenger kilometres (km)	37	50	+ 35.1
Passenger journeys (millions)	761	1 014	+ 33.3
Passenger revenue (£ million)[1]	2 379	3 893	+ 63.6
Goods moved (billion tonne km)	13	20	+ 53.8
Goods lifted (million tonnes)	92[2]	89	- 3.3
Investment in national rail system (£ million)[3]	900	4 265	+ 373.9
Investment in rail rolling stock (£ million)[3]	200	566[4]	+ 183.0
Subsidies[3]	1 741	3 622	+ 108.0

Notes:
[1] Current prices
[2] Data refers to 1998 due to reclassification
[3] Outturn prices
[4] Data for 2002/03

Source: Transport Statistics, Great Britain (various)

Bargain fares have been used to fill spare off-peak capacity. For example, in September 2005 GNER were offering an off-peak bargain return fare from Leeds to London Kings Cross for just £19 – if you could get one! The standard class open return was a whacking £149. Cheaper saver and business saver returns were also available but were subject to travel limitations. For example, the latter was only available for outward travel after 8 am.

This form of pricing is indicative of a travel market that can be segmented by the train operator in order to maximise revenue. The peak period is one where the price elasticity of demand is inelastic – a figure of -0.4 is typical. For the off-peak, the fare elasticity is price elastic, typically -1.1. This relatively high figure seems reasonable because of the optional nature of many types of off-peak travel.

Figure 5 shows the case of a price discriminating monopolist. If the monopolist were to charge a single price where MC=MR, then a loss equal to the shaded area would be made. By applying the principle of third degree price discrimination, the monopolist is taking the view that some travellers are prepared to pay above P_1, for example business travellers who have to travel to a business meeting in London. Where the price exceeds P_1, then the monopolist is seeking to reduce consumer surplus. By converting this

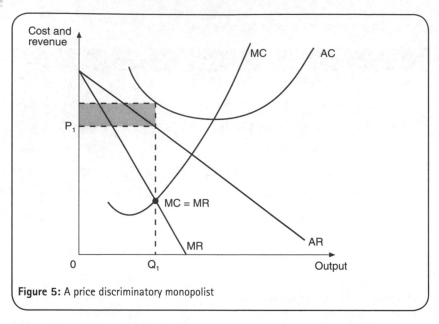

Figure 5: A price discriminatory monopolist

into producer surplus, the monopolist is seeking to maximise revenue and generate excess profits.

If I ran the railways

Stelios Haji-Ioannou, founder of the no-frills flight company easyJet and easyGroup

'I don't believe I could fix Britain's railways. It's a very different situation to running an airline. Setting up a private airline is a normal commercial venture. Running the rail industry is a government task.

'The first difference - and problem - is that, by their very nature, airlines are free to move around whereas with the railway's track system, the freedom to move is limited. How do you create competition in the railway business, short of having two parallel tracks going to the same place?

'As far as efficiency is concerned, the reason easyJet became so efficient was by using the net for ticketing. I know you can book train tickets online, but the devil's in the detail. Some sites are incredibly efficient and some aren't.'

Source: The Guardian, 15 January 2002

A commuter's tale

Joann Cooper, Legal PA
Enfield Town to Liverpool Street

I take the train every working day to Liverpool Street and then go by tube to Chancery Lane where my office is. It's only a 35-minute journey into Liverpool Street but it is often horrendous.

Before Christmas it was especially bad. I sometimes had to wait an hour for a train. Because I get on at the start of the line I do tend to get a seat but by the time the train leaves it is usually full and people at the next stations have to fight to get on. Tempers get frayed.

There is also a problem if the train before the one I catch is cancelled. The platform can then be packed and it's a scramble to find a seat. They come up with all sorts of reasons – the driver has not turned up or there are problems with the points.

I buy a weekly travelcard which costs £34. Over the year that's quite a lot of money if you can't even get a seat. I have to aim to get an earlier train so I've a better chance of getting to work on time.

Source: The Guardian, 15 January 2002

This principle is one that underpinned GNER's successful bid in 2005 to retain its East Coast main line franchise for a further 10 years. GNER has experienced commercial success; it has also run a well-managed franchise. The cost of retaining its franchise though, has not come cheap – it is estimated that GNER will be making a premium payment averaging £130 million per year, or £1.3 billon over the 10 year period. Revenue growth for GNER has been healthy and the company believe that by improving the quality of the product, further growth will be generated. The uncertainty and risk come about if traffic growth falls below target, in which case costs will have to be reduced and the already expensive fares increased.

Prior to privatisation, the national rail network suffered badly in terms of underinvestment and neglect from central government. In part this was due to the lack of a positive commitment to rail's future role in the transport network. Privatisation has reversed this. Investment funding has come from four main sources, Network Rail, train operating companies, financial institutions and railway rolling stock companies. The scale of new investment that has followed privatisation is far in excess of what the public sector would have been able to fund if Britain's railways had remained nationalised. This has been a very positive outcome of privatisation.

Rail privatisation is not without its critics, though. Together, expenditure for Network Rail and current expenditure for revenue support represent a massive expense for the taxpayer. In all, central and local government are spending around £60 per head per annum on the rail network...whether people travel by train or not!

The Public Performance Measure (PPM) is a measure of the percentage of trains arriving on time, combining former separate measures of punctuality and reliability. A train is defined as being 'on time' if it arrives within five minutes of its planned destination time (London, South East and regional operators) or 10 minutes on long distance operations. Tables 7 and 8 provide some interesting statistics. As they show, performance is steadily improving, although punctuality still remains below what it was at the time of the Hatfield disaster. The main reason for the improvement has to be the massive infrastructure investment programme being carried out by Network Rail. Further advances could be made if some of the train operating companies were to invest more in rolling stock and staffing.

Although as shown above, some passengers have benefited from cheap fare deals, others have not. This is particularly the case for business travellers and some season ticket holders for whom the rise in rail fares has consistently been in excess of the underlying rate of inflation.

Another criticism of privatisation has concerned safety. There is a view that safety is being compromised by a lack of spending and poor management control. Although perception has improved, after the Hatfield disaster especially, there has been a loss of confidence in the industry and in the standards of maintenance by contractors (as the cartoon demonstrates). Network Rail has now decided to undertake much of its own maintenance.

Source: Daily Telegraph, 21 December 2003

Table 7: PPM 1997/98–2004/05

Year	% trains arriving on time
1997/98	89.7
1998/99	87.9
1999/00	87.8
2000/01	(post-Hatfield) 79.1
2001/02	78.0
2002/03	79.2
2003/04	81.2
2004/05	84.3

Table 8: Best and worst performers 2004/05

	% trains arriving on time		% trains arriving on time
c2c	93.9	First Great Western	67.8
Merseyrail	92.6	GNER	71.8
South West Trains	88.7	Transpennine Express	75.1
Northern Rail	87.6	Arriva Trains Wales	76.7

Source: Network Rail, 2005

Within the wider context of national transport policy, the privatised railway industry is required:

- to provide a cost-effective and safe railway
- to be able to offer travellers of all kinds a realistic choice of transport mode
- to be able to carry much more freight
- to make a significant contribution to reducing road congestion and environmental pollution.

To date, the private railway industry has made a contribution towards these objectives. It is though, struggling to meet its targets and will continue to do so unless further private sector investment can be generated. There is also a clear need to keep costs under control and to continue to enhance public confidence by addressing on-going worries over safety.

Summary

On completion of this chapter, you have learnt that:

- transport markets consist of a series of sub-markets

- excluding perfect competition, evidence can be compiled to show that in overall terms, many transport markets are oligopolostic

- there are various types of barrier to entry into transport markets and the strength of these invariably determines the degree of competition in a given market

- the threat of potential new firms entering an industry is an important requirement if contestability is to be achieved in a market

- despite deregulation, the market for local bus services in Britain has continued to decline except for London, where passenger numbers have increased due to the increased frequency of bus provision (see the section entitled *Deregulation – local bus services in Britain* on page 55)

- in contrast, the deregulation of European air services has produced substantial benefits and changes

- the privatisation of transport is a controversial issue, with arguments for as well as against

- the privatisation of the rail network has produced winners and losers.

Useful websites

Institute of Economic Affairs www.iea.org.uk

Strategic Rail Authority www.sra.gov.uk (note: no longer being updated)

Activities

Topics for investigation

1. Consider the local bus market where you live.

    a) Find out which firms operate, how long they have been in the market, what fares they charge, how big they are and so on.

    b) Use all the information you have collected to assess the extent to which your local bus market is contestable.

2. In 2004, the First Group took over the ScotRail franchise from National Express after an investigation by the Office of Fair Trade (OFT). Use the internet to find out about the OFT's concerns and discuss the advantages and disadvantages of the eventual outcome.

Exam-style practice questions

Data response question

1. Study the data provided in the section entitled *European logistics providers* on page 59 and then answer the following questions:

   a) What evidence is there to suggest that the European logistics industry is an oligopoly? (4)

   b) Would you expect the degree of concentration to increase or decrease in the future? Justify your answer. (4)

   c) Explain how European logistics providers might compete with each other. (6)

Essay questions

1. a) Explain the relationship between the component parts within the structure of the UK railway industry. (10)

   b) Discuss the ways in which economists might assess the efficiency of the UK railway industry. (15)

   (OCR, Module 2885, January 2005)

2. Following deregulation of the European air transport industry, low-cost airlines have entered the market to provide cheaper alternatives to traditional carriers.

   a) Explain how firms compete in monopolistic competition. (10)

   b) Discuss the extent to which the structure of the European air transport industry has been affected by the entry of low-cost airlines. (15)

   (OCR, Module 2885, January 2004)

3. In October 2003, proposals were introduced to reverse the deregulation of the local bus industry in order to reduce problems caused by some local monopolies within the industry.

   a) Explain the main problems associated with monopolies. (10)

   b) Discuss the possible impact of greater regulation on the local bus industry in the UK. (15)

5 Traffic congestion and policies for combating traffic congestion

In this chapter, you will learn:

- what is meant by congestion
- how economists estimate the costs of road congestion
- what policy options are available for combating road congestion
- what is meant by road pricing and user charging
- why congestion is a classic case of market failure
- why some form of road pricing is the only proven and effective way of reducing congestion in many towns and cities
- about the experience of UK cities and others where road pricing schemes have been implemented.

> **Key words** congestion • external cost • indirect cost
> Lorry Road User Charge • marginal private benefit
> marginal social benefit • market failure • road pricing
> user charging

The problem of congestion

Congestion is an all too familiar feature of most transport networks. It occurs where there is too much traffic relative to capacity: in other words, where demand exceeds supply. The result is that:

- actual journey times are greater than expected
- the cost of making a trip is greater than it should be
- for freight users, more vehicles are needed for a particular volume of work
- there is a greater use of fuel and more extensive vehicle emissions than if traffic were flowing freely, which represents an ineffective use of scarce resources.

Congestion is normally associated with the road network and although this will be the focus of this chapter, it should be recognised that congestion is experienced in all forms of transport at the present time. For example, the capacity of Heathrow Airport is such that when airline slots become vacant

they are traded on the market. Sections of the mainline rail network and slots into major stations are fully taken up. Massive new investment is needed to improve the situation.

Congestion is not new. In ancient Rome, chariots were prohibited from using the streets between daylight and dusk owing to serious congestion problems. In the UK, London and other cities suffered from congestion long before the coming of the motor car. What is new, however, is the scale of the problem of congestion – many of our principal motorways and routes are heavily congested for large parts of the day. At times it is becoming increasingly difficult to identify peak and off-peak periods, particularly on the roads. The Commission for Integrated Transport has carried out research which shows that the UK has the worst congested roads in the EU15 (see Figure 1).

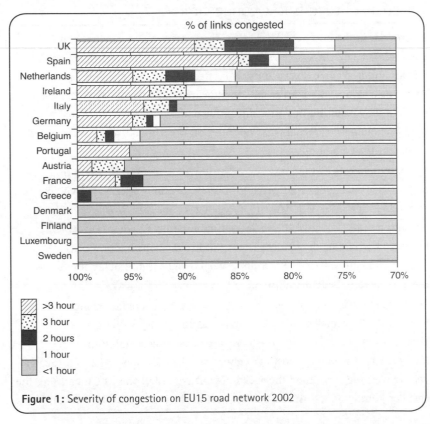

Figure 1: Severity of congestion on EU15 road network 2002

Users on almost a quarter of the most well used road links suffered regular delays lasting an hour or more. In Germany and France, such delays were suffered on less than one in ten links and in some countries, there were no links where this level of delay was being experienced. The Commission attributed this woeful situation to:

- persistent under-investment in the road network over many years (see also Chapter 3)
- heavy reliance on the private car as a means of transport, despite having below EU average car ownership levels
- the extensive use of the car for the journey to work.

It should also be recognised that road congestion is not confined to developed economies such as the UK, France, the USA and so on. Far from it – some of the most serious road congestion problems can be found in the emerging economies of South East Asia (see *Traffic Congestion in Bangkok and Beijing* on page 79).

The costs of road traffic congestion

At present, in the absence of a market, road space is allocated through queuing. The current system, whereby users pay high indirect taxes on fuel and an annual vehicle excise duty, is ineffective in combating congestion. As a consequence, the market fails to allocate scarce resources in the most efficient way resulting in various negative externalities. The outcome is that road users impose external costs not only on other road users but on other groups in the community as well.

The **external costs** of road traffic congestion are shown in Figure 2 on page 80. If D is the demand curve for travel, then at a price P_1 per vehicle kilometre, road users will demand Q_1 vehicle kilometres. This level of demand though, is above the social optimum point, E_s, where Q_2 vehicle kilometres would be demanded. The result is over-consumption of Q_1-Q_2 vehicle kilometres, with the **marginal social benefit** (MSB) being less than the **marginal private benefit** (MPB).

The marginal costs of congestion can be shown by a simple example. Suppose 1 000 vehicles are travelling along an urban road at say 15 kilometres per hour and that this is regarded as an acceptable speed by their drivers. Assume the cost per vehicle for their journey is £2. If a further vehicle uses the road, then the speed of traffic will fall slightly, increasing the cost per journey to £2.01. The private cost of the journey to the new driver is

Case study: Traffic congestion in Bangkok and Beijing

Bangkok's congestion problems are well documented. Every day almost three million vehicles try to battle their way through the Thai capital's over-stretched and over-used road network. The result is that Bangkok is clogged with vehicles that belt out a daily cocktail of black exhaust fumes and unacceptable levels of noise pollution. Bangkok's drivers spend the equivalent of 22 days a year in their vehicles. It is not unknown for a two mile journey in the rush hour to take hours. Children often leave home at 4 am to beat the traffic...and go back to bed when they reach their schools!

There are though, signs of change. Bangkok's elevated Skytrain opened in 2001, although the network is limited and fares are high. A new underground system has been completed, residents can obtain traffic information on their PC's and part of the city centre has now been pedestrianised in an attempt to improve the city's appalling traffic congestion and pollution levels. Bus lanes, co-ordinated traffic light systems and a better one-way traffic system have also been introduced. All of this might seem bad news for the city's 'white knuckle riders', motorcyclists who risk the lives of their pillion passengers as they weave their way through the endless jams of traffic. Things have undoubtedly got better but not sufficiently so as to force these daredevils off the streets.

Traffic congestion is a prominent problem in Beijing, with car ownership levels rising by 10 per cent annually in recent years. Cars seem to be overwhelming Beijing – peoples' incomes are increasing and the price of vehicles decreasing in real terms. The problem is that the road network has not been developed to match the increase in traffic growth. The air quality and environmental conditions in the central area are desperately poor...and deteriorating.

The municipal government has found it necessary to take a radical look at relieving congestion through decentralisation. This involves setting up new urban sub centres around the city in order to reduce the total demand for access into the city centre. This is, however, a long term strategy. In the short term, the policies that are being tried include increasing the cost of car parking, improvements to some roads to increase capacity, a better underground mass transit system and interestingly, a cut back in the number of taxis.

£2.01, the same as to all other drivers. The marginal external cost imposed on other drivers is £10, or 1000 x one penny. The marginal social cost though, is £10 plus the private costs of £2.01, making £12.01 in total. Even from this simple example it is easy to see why the costs of traffic congestion are substantial on heavily congested roads.

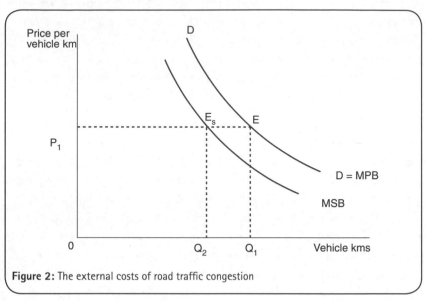

Figure 2: The external costs of road traffic congestion

Various estimates have been made of the costs of road traffic congestion to the British economy. The CBI, for example, estimate the cost to be well above £20 billion a year and increasing. A high proportion of this total comes from value of time costs (see Chapter 3). Other items cover the direct user costs as shown by the simple numerical example above. Less obvious, and not included in the CBI's estimate, are the hidden costs to individuals and businesses in the form of increased strain and stress, the need for more vehicles to do the same volume of work and the additional logistics costs incurred by firms having to hold more inventory than would be the case if their supply chains could operate efficiently.

These **indirect costs** of traffic congestion are shown in Figure 3. As this indicates, increased traffic congestion will inevitably have adverse effects on logistics service providers. Although some of the costs can be internalised through the more efficient management of warehouses and fleets of trucks, a major incident such as a serious road accident or motorway lane closure, can have a profound effect on the costs and efficiency of the operation.

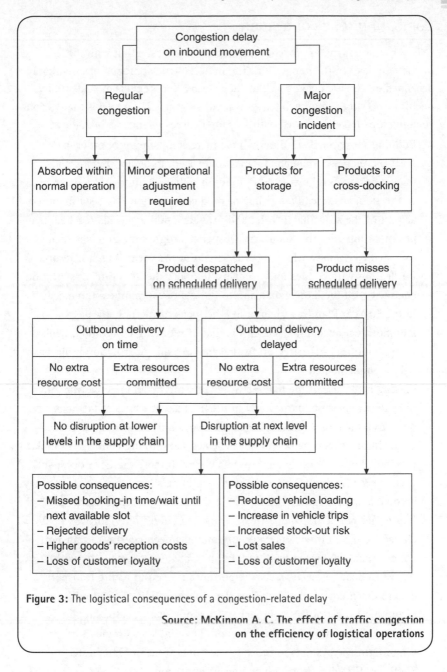

Figure 3: The logistical consequences of a congestion-related delay

Source: McKinnon A. C. The effect of traffic congestion
on the efficiency of logistical operations

Combating road congestion

Over the years, many approaches have been used for dealing with the problem of road traffic congestion. The nature of the approach has invariably depended on the political as well as the transport context. That said, at any one time, no single approach has prevailed; what has happened is that various combinations have been tried with varying degrees of success including:

- Building more roads. In other words, increasing supply in order to meet the increase in demand. This would seem to be an obvious and logical policy to follow whether it be for relieving inter-urban or urban congestion. Historically, a policy of road construction has been favoured as part of the so-called 'predict and provide' approach. This reached its peak in 1989 with the Roads for Prosperity programme and was then followed by a phase when new road building was seen as a last resort for dealing with congestion problems. In 2000, the government's attitude changed with the large expansion to the road programme announced in the 10 Year Plan (see Chapter 6). The focus of the new by-passes and motorway widening schemes is that of relieving congestion, whilst recognising that hereafter, no further major road construction projects will be implemented.

- Making better use of the road network. This can be an effective way of reducing congestion, particularly in urban areas. All sorts of methods have been used including creating urban clearways and bus lanes, improved traffic light systems, park and ride schemes, car parking controls, workplace parking charges, priority lanes for vehicles with more than one occupant, cycle lanes and so on. These methods tend to be short term is so far as they involve making a more efficient use of the existing road infrastructure.

- Improving public transport. This approach involves providing a realistic choice for urban travellers especially and has been central to transport policy since 1997 (see Chapter 6). Public transport, particularly with regard to buses, is seen as very important in meeting future transport demand in many towns and cities. The subsidisation of local rail services is another aspect of this approach. A lack of private sector support though, will continue to limit the capital available to provide further urban light rail systems to those already operating in Manchester, Sheffield, Croydon, Nottingham and Birmingham.

- Charging systems. There is now a consensus amongst economists that there is only one way of relieving the problem of urban congestion, namely bringing prices more into line with costs, and therefore increasing the cost of vehicle use in urban areas. Road pricing was first recommended in 1964 as the way forward for relieving congestion and then again, in 1971. It is now central to the government's strategy for the future of transport in Britain, as the rest of this chapter will show.

What is meant by road pricing?

In June 2005, after eight years of debate and dithering, the government finally announced its plans to introduce a national system of **road pricing** to replace the current indirect way in which road users pay for the use of road space. The principle underpinning road pricing is simple – road users pay according to when, where and how much they use the road network. To the economist, this at last is a way of addressing the problem of **market failure** arising from the ever-growing problem of traffic congestion, since the cost of congestion is ascribed to those responsible for causing it.

Economists have argued for a long time that the price mechanism could be used to ration the supply of road space in the same way that it is used to ration most other scarce resources. After all, as stated earlier, congestion is a situation where the demand for roadspace in certain parts of the network at particular times exceeds the capacity or supply that is available. Moreover, as well as reducing congestion, road pricing has the additional important quality that revenue generated can be used to invest in quality public transport alternatives.

How is user charging different?

In recent years, the terms **user charging** and congestion charging have been used. In many respects, these are no different to road pricing, apart from being seemingly less painful to those who have to pay! Strictly speaking, road pricing implies that the cost to the user can be accurately determined. A user charge or congestion charge in contrast is a flat rate charge levied for access into a designated zone or cordon (see *London Congestion Charge*). This is a much blunter way of collecting a direct payment from road users.

Congestion: a classic case of market failure

Figures 4 and 5 on pages 84 and 85 show the basic principles underpinning road pricing. Figure 4 shows the classic market failure situation. Here, the cost paid by road users, P_p, is below the social optimum of P_s. As a consequence, their use of the road network is above the social optimum. The distance between Q_s and Q_p represents this over-use. External costs not paid for by road users are shown by the shaded area, sometimes known as the welfare loss triangle. When these external costs are internalised through the introduction of road pricing, the MPC shifts upwards until it passes through the social optimum point where MPC=MSC and MPB=MSB. The new equilibrium position is shown in Figure 5.

Case study: London Congestion Charge

The London Congestion Charge (LCC) was introduced in February 2003. Set initially at £5 per day, it was increased to £8 in July 2005. It has the following key features:

- All vehicles that are used in the charging zone have to pay the charge, except for vehicles such as emergency vehicles, taxis, alternative energy vehicles and blue/orange badge holders.
- Residents within the zone receive a 90 per cent discount; fleet users pay £7 per day.
- The charge is active from 07.00 to 18.30, Monday to Friday, excluding public holidays.
- There are various ways of paying the charge including the internet, telephone, text message or in person at a designated retail outlet. Weekly, monthly and annual passes are available, the latter two providing discounts.
- The scheme is managed by a network of cameras that read vehicle registration plates.
- If the charge is not paid by midnight on the day that it is incurred, there is a £100 fine levied. This reduces to £40 if payment is made within 14 days.
- The charging zone currently extends from King's Cross in the north to Elephant and Castle in the south and from Vauxhall Bridge in the west to Tower Bridge in the east. In September 2005 it was announced that the zone will be extended westwards to cover a similar area. Charging here will start in February 2007. At the same time, the charging time period will finish at 18.00 and there will be some minor concessions for late payers. The plans to extend to include Knightsbridge, Kensington and Chelsea have been vigorously opposed by business leaders, residents and motoring organisations.

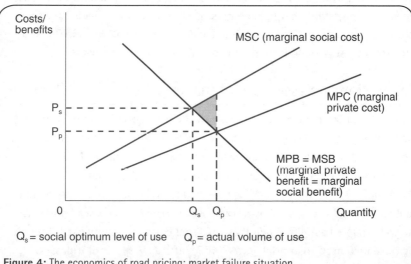

Q_s = social optimum level of use Q_p = actual volume of use

Figure 4: The economics of road pricing: market failure situation

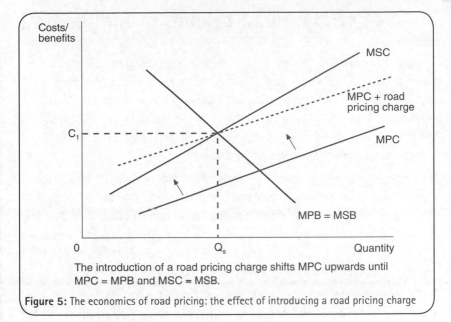

The introduction of a road pricing charge shifts MPC upwards until MPC = MPB and MSC = MSB.

Figure 5: The economics of road pricing: the effect of introducing a road pricing charge

The assumption made is that the road pricing charge can be estimated accurately so as to internalise the full cost of the negative externality. This is fine in theory but difficult to apply in practice due to:

- problems associated with calculating the true costs of negative externalities – even with a complex system such as that operating in Singapore (see *Electronic road pricing in Singapore*) it is difficult to determine what the charges should be
- problems of knowing where to draw the boundary for any charging zone (see *London Congestion Charge*); for a national system, this is not necessarily a problem
- problems associated with visitors, occasional users and residents in the charging zone
- problems of public acceptance.

A user charge involves a direct approach. Looking at Figures 4 and 5 again, the introduction of a flat-rate user charge will shift the MPC line upwards, not necessarily to where it fully intersects with the MSC line.

The pros and cons of road pricing

There are various benefits of road pricing:

- It has now been shown to be effective in reducing congestion levels. It reduces traffic volumes, increases traffic speeds and improves efficiency.

Case study: Road pricing in Singapore

Singapore has had a form of road pricing since 1975. The original manual system, known as the Area Licensing System (ALS), required the owners of vehicles being used in the 'restricted zone' to purchase and display a licence entitling them to use their vehicles between 07.30 and 19.00 on weekdays and up to 14.00 on Saturdays. Enforcement was at the entry point – any vehicles not displaying a valid licence were identified and a summons sent to their owners.

The Electronic Road Pricing system (ERP) replaced the above in 1998. All vehicles are required to be fitted with an in-vehicle unit that holds a smart card called CashCard. When the vehicle is used in the charging zone, units are deducted depending on traffic volumes and the time that the vehicle is used in this zone. The CashCard can be topped up at petrol stations or at a network of automatic teller machines. Unlike the ALS, the ERP system requires motorists to pay every time they enter the charging zone.

The ERP is seen by the Singapore government as a fair, convenient and reliable means of charging for the use of roadspace in the restricted zone. It is further argued that it offers residents a realistic choice, namely whether to use their car, pool with others or travel by the efficient MRT or public bus network that has been funded by the revenue generated by road pricing.

The impact of ERP on congestion has been:

- a reduction of peak period traffic by 16 per cent in the first year of operation
- vehicle speeds of 20–30 kilometres per hour on arterial roads, an improvement on earlier speeds, in line with desired optimal speeds
- an increase in vehicles entering the restricted zone before charging starts and after it ends.

- Given that roadspace is underpriced and overused, it is a relevant way of correcting market failure. In many respects, to the economist, this is the principal advantage of road pricing. The reduction in congestion, while welcome, is the outcome of correcting market failure.
- Revenue from road pricing can be hypothecated into new transport projects such as new road developments or in the case of London, additional bus services, subsidised public transport fares and improvements to the Underground.

Despite the attractiveness of the above arguments, road pricing has its critics, and there are numerous arguments against such schemes, including:

- The present system of taxation on road users through fuel duty and vehicle excise duty is well established, well understood and easy to enforce – so why change it?
- Road pricing is regressive and is likely to have the most significant impact on low income road users. This raises all sorts of equity issues.
- Road pricing is not popular with large sections of the community. To be effective, road pricing must be accepted by the public and recognised as the only realistic solution to the congestion problems they are facing.
- Estimating the level of charge is by no means easy and to be effective, must be at a rate where it will reduce the demand for roadspace.
- Although the technology for charging is now proven, the means and costs of tracking and following up non-payers can be a serious drain on the revenue that is generated from a road pricing charge.

A national system of road pricing for Britain

In June 2005, the Transport Secretary, Alistair Darling, announced the government's plans for a national 'pay as you drive' system of charging for the use of roadspace in Britain. If the plans materialise, it will be by far the biggest and most ambitious road pricing scheme that has ever been attempted (see Figure 6). In proposing this radical policy, Mr Darling warned that it was essential if the country were to avoid a Los Angeles style gridlock in the near future.

The basic points about the system are:

- The charge could be as high as £1.30 per mile for using the busiest, most congested roads during peak periods. This charge would typically apply to stretches of roads into major cities and on motorways such as the M25 and congested parts of the M1, M4, M6 and M62.
- Elsewhere, the charge will be much lower and could be as little as two pence per mile on deserted rural roads. A more typical charge might be 10–15 pence per mile for most urban journeys.
- The intention is that the scheme could be 'tax neutral' in so far as it would merely replace the present system of fuel duty and vehicle excise duty and not add to the total taxation that is paid to the Treasury by road users. This would though, be a redistribution of what road users pay, with an estimated 15–20 per cent paying more than at present. These users would largely be regular car commuters into major cities and towns.
- Before going ahead, there is to be a full scale trial in one city: Bristol or Manchester has been suggested.
- It is estimated that the system could be up and running by 2015.

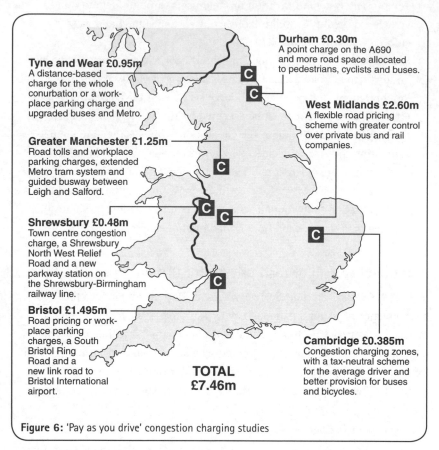

Tyne and Wear £0.95m
A distance-based charge for the whole conurbation or a workplace parking charge and upgraded buses and Metro.

Durham £0.30m
A point charge on the A690 and more road space allocated to pedestrians, cyclists and buses.

West Midlands £2.60m
A flexible road pricing scheme with greater control over private bus and rail companies.

Greater Manchester £1.25m
Road tolls and workplace parking charges, extended Metro tram system and guided busway between Leigh and Salford.

Shrewsbury £0.48m
Town centre congestion charge, a Shrewsbury North West Relief Road and a new parkway station on the Shrewsbury-Birmingham railway line.

Bristol £1.495m
Road pricing or workplace parking charges, a South Bristol Ring Road and a new link road to Bristol International airport.

Cambridge £0.385m
Congestion charging zones, with a tax-neutral scheme for the average driver and better provision for buses and bicycles.

TOTAL £7.46m

Figure 6: 'Pay as you drive' congestion charging studies

Figure 7 shows the two main charging systems that are being considered. The 'tag and beacon' system operates effectively in Singapore (see *Road pricing in Singapore* on page 86) and variations on it have been successfully used in other places. It can be used with a smart card whereby a device is fitted to a vehicle's dashboard and the driver can see just how much is being charged for using the vehicle. This is proven technology – its downside is the huge capital cost involved in erecting a network of gantries throughout the country as well as tagging approximately 30 million vehicles. A second system, using GPS satellite technology, is also being assessed. This uses the same principle as the tracking systems that are fitted to goods vehicles and navigation systems that are increasingly being fitted to more expensive cars. At present, there are problems relating to the strength of signal, particularly in some cities, although such problems seem likely to be resolved, making this system a very attractive practical proposition, avoiding some of the capital costs of the tag and beacon method.

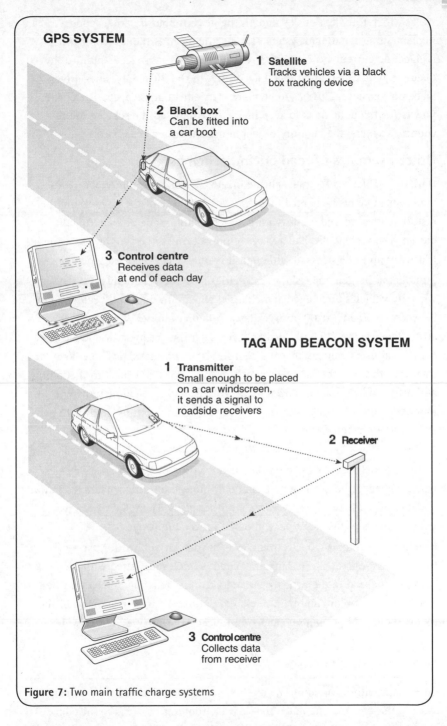

GPS SYSTEM

1 Satellite
Tracks vehicles via a black
box tracking device

2 Black box
Can be fitted into
a car boot

3 Control centre
Receives data
at end of each day

TAG AND BEACON SYSTEM

1 Transmitter
Small enough to be placed
on a car windscreen,
it sends a signal to
roadside receivers

2 Receiver

3 Control centre
Collects data
from receiver

Figure 7: Two main traffic charge systems

At last, therefore, it seems as though the government is serious about implementing a national system of road pricing in Britain. If so, it will replace the current system, whereby the nation's roadspace is rationed by queuing, with one that rations it according to the different values drivers place on journeys. This has to be more efficient in all respects. The challenge now is for the politicians to keep their nerve and sell the scheme to the country's voters, the majority of whom are frustrated road users.

Other examples of road pricing schemes

Durham – This was the first scheme in the UK where, from October 2002, motorists have been charged £2 to exit a small area of the city around the historic cathedral and castle, with payment being made at an automatic barrier. The scheme has had a massive impact on congestion levels, reducing traffic by up to 85 per cent, although it is only a very modest scheme.

Trondheim, Bergen and Oslo – These cities all have very similar systems, whereby vehicles are tagged and charged when entering a city centre zone between 06.00 and 18.00 on weekdays. A higher charge is applied before 10.00. Electronic toll booths deduct a fee each time a tagged vehicle passes; occasional users can pay by card or cash at an automatic machine. Regular users pay through their bank accounts or by making a deposit to the tolling authority. Toll revenue has been used to fund road and public transport improvements and peak hour traffic volumes have fallen by around 10 per cent on the pre-toll situation.

Toronto – This is the site of the world's first all-electronic highway charging system. Vehicles are charged on the distance travelled, with most vehicles being tagged, although some are charged through a licence plate recognition system. Billing is retrospective on a monthly basis. There have been major improvements in journey time compared to free highways.

Melbourne – Since 2000, electronic tolls have been applied for users of the privately-operated City Link Toll Road. Vehicles are fitted with pre-paid e-tags fitted to the windscreen and accounts must be topped up when credit reaches a minimum point. Less regular users can pay by noon of the following day. Major improvements in journey times have been recorded.

Lorry road user charging

Coincident with its announcements for the planned national road pricing system, the government stated that it was dropping its plans to introduce a **Lorry Road User Charge** (LRUC) in 2008. This significant step serves to reinforce the government's commitment to national road pricing, although the transport industry is not pleased that the LRUC has, for the time being at least, been scrapped.

The idea behind the LRUC was to ensure that foreign-owned trucks made a fair contribution to the costs they impose on the road network when being used in the UK. At present, many are free riders in so far as they do not purchase diesel fuel in the UK and do not therefore pay any taxes to the Treasury. This is seen as unfair because it means that UK haulers cannot compete on an equal basis with those from abroad, where fuel is much cheaper.

The road freight market in the EU has been fully liberalised since 1997. The problem is that no harmonised system of taxation exists to provide a 'level playing field' and ensure fair competition. The taxation on diesel fuel, that can be around 35 per cent of total costs, varies enormously. It is highest in the UK, typically 20 pence per litre more than elsewhere in the EU. A LRUC would have rectified this problem.

Elsewhere in Europe, Switzerland, Austria and most recently, the German 'maut' system, charge foreign haulers to use their road and motorway networks. The UK road transport industry had been critical of the government's plans to tax all goods vehicles through the LRUC, claiming that it was unlikely to be tax neutral as far as UK haulers were concerned. This is now history and for the time being, provides little consolation for the UK's hard-pressed transport and logistics companies.

Summary

On completion of this chapter, you have learnt that:

- congestion, particularly road congestion, is a serious problem affecting the efficiency of transport networks in many countries

- current indirect systems of taxation do little to discourage congestion

- the market fails to allocate resources in an efficient way when there is congestion

- building new roads, improving traffic management and improving public transport can improve urban road congestion

- a proven and effective long term approach to combating congestion is some form of road pricing

- a national system of road pricing represents a new radical approach to addressing this case of market failure.

Useful websites

Independent Transport Commission www.trg.soton.ac.uk

BBC News www.bbc.co.uk

Activities

Topics for investigation

1. Re-draw Figure 4 to show how the equilibrium position is affected by the introduction of a flat rate user charge such as the London Congestion Charge that covers some but not all of the costs of negative externalities. Compare this with the diagram in Figure 5.

2. Using the Internet and other sources, see what information you can find on whether other UK cities, apart from London and Durham, plan to introduce road user charges. (Hint: try Cardiff and Nottingham.) Also, see what you can find out about why Edinburgh residents have rejected a road user charge.

Exam-style practice questions

Essay questions

1. In July 2006 the London Congestion Charge increased from £5 to £8 per day. According to Transport for London, the number of drivers paying the congestion charge has fallen by 'no more than 2000 per day' from a typical day's figure of 80 000. What might you conclude about the price elasticity of demand for travel into the charging zone? What are the implications for transport policies in London? (25)

2. Discuss the view that 'a national system of road pricing would undermine arguments for subsidising rail passenger services and put rural railway lines at risk'. (25)

3. Following the introduction of the congestion charge in London in 2003, there have been many suggestions for the introduction of user charging in other UK cities.

    a) Explain the economic basis for road user charging in cites. (10)

    b) Discuss the likely impact on businesses of widespread road user charging in the UK. (15)

(OCR, Module 2885, June 2005)

6 From transport economics to transport policies

In this chapter, you will learn about:

- the relationship between transport economics and transport policies, particularly in the UK
- the objectives of transport policy
- the nature and features of an integrated transport policy
- the role of government and the market in the allocation of resources in the transport sector
- how and why the private sector has increasingly funded transport projects
- why the 'best allocation of resources' may not always be possible and why this may constitute market failure
- why there is a growing consensus among economists that transport policy should be promoting more sustainable transport outcomes.

> **Key words** accessibility • co-ordination • hypothecation integration • government failure • public-private partnership social exclusion • sustainable transport

The objectives of transport policy

From a simplistic standpoint, the objective of transport policy should be to ensure that there is the 'best or most efficient allocation of resources' in the transport sector. Because of the nature of the transport function (see Chapter 1), in practice, this is very difficult to achieve. As a consequence, the UK does not have a single comprehensive transport policy that covers all modes of transport, passengers and freight included. What we do have is a range of transport policies that from time-to-time are co-ordinated by governments into an all-embracing set of policy statements, the most recent of which is 'The Future of Transport' (Department for Transport, 2004), details of which will be analysed at the end of this chapter.

Figure 1 shows the broad framework or context for transport policy in the UK. The approach of the various Conservative governments from 1979 to 1997 was to use market forces to improve the allocation of resources by releasing the restraint of public sector organisation and control. Deregulation and privatisation were the means by which this was achieved (see Chapter 4).

The means were to:

- increase competition in the provision of bus, rail, air and road freight services
- establish new structures that would maintain the public interest in this important sector of the economy
- ensure better 'value for money' for public sector expenditure and at the same time, direct public sector investment to where it was most needed.

Transport policy in this period could not be divorced from the wider political ideology of reducing the role of government in the affairs of the economy. The strategic objective of transport policy at the end of this period was stated as being one of providing 'an efficient and competitive transport market to serve the interests of the economy and community, with maximum emphasis on safety and the environment'. Despite its generality, the aim was predominantly economic. It also provided clear signals that the price mechanism was being used to not only allocate resources but also to make clear to both providers and consumers the true costs of providing transport services.

Despite what it may have said while in opposition, the incoming Labour government of 1997 was limited in what it could do to the structure of transport provision. The Conservative legislation had made it impossible for the privatisation process to be reversed. Labour's transport policy has nevertheless continued the theme of promoting greater efficiency in the use of scarce resources, for road and rail especially, while emphasising the need for transport policy to:

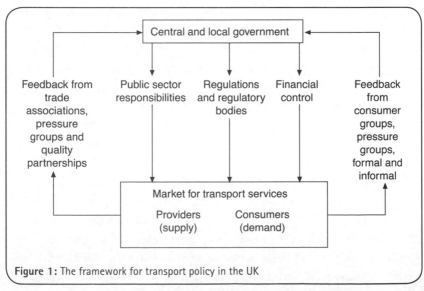

Figure 1: The framework for transport policy in the UK

- promote environmental objectives, particularly with respect to meeting obligations to the Kyoto protocol
- reduce **social exclusion** as a consequence of poor transport provision by improving the **accessibility** of all groups to transport services
- ensure that there is real choice for users of passenger and freight transport services
- enhance the vitality of town and city centres, while meeting the needs of those living in rural areas
- promote a greater awareness of transport issues throughout society.

Towards an integrated transport policy

Co-ordination has for a long time been an objective of transport policy. For many years, successive governments sought to achieve this through creating competitive conditions whereby co-ordination would occur through the natural workings of the market mechanism. **Integration** is rather different in the sense that it is an objective that is specifically achieved through measures that are put in place by central and local government working closely together to link all aspects of transport to produce a single total system. Strictly speaking, therefore, an integrated transport policy should seek to do this for all forms of transport infrastructure. It can also be seen as a way of eliminating **government failure** in transport policy whereby a policy pursued for one mode of transport is at variance with that being followed for another mode.

As part of its fundamental review of transport policy, the Labour government made its intentions clear in a consultation document called 'Developing an Integrated Transport Policy'. This document pursued an integrated transport policy that had a strong commitment to an environmentally **sustainable transport** system. It represented a radical change in direction of national transport policy.

The main reason for change was the forecasted growth in road traffic. In the absence of a change in policy, and hence travel habits, road traffic was expected to grow by between 37 and 57 per cent by 2017. Even at the bottom end, the message was a clear one – a massive increase in road traffic congestion (see chapter 5). The government was also concerned, as stated above, to include a more explicit social and environmental dimension to transport policy by providing a real choice for those who were being denied it through the ever-increasing use of road transport. Such groups included:

- Non-car owners. Although approaching 70 per cent of households had a car available, 30 per cent did not have a car and amongst car-owning households, there were members of the family who had to rely on public transport for many of their transport needs. The elderly and low-income families especially were increasingly finding their lives affected by inadequate access to transport.

- Those living outside major towns and cities. A consequence of deregulation was that many unremunerative bus services had been withdrawn, particularly that were off-peak or outside the main centres of population.
- Many freight users, for whom road transport was the only choice available. More was clearly needed to encourage a greater use of rail freight services by business.

Achieving better integration can come about in various ways. At a local level, one of the most common complaints from public transport users is that services are unstructured and badly linked. This has been one of the unfortunate consequences of deregulation (see Chapter 4). A locally integrated public transport policy can help through providing:

- better information for passengers, for example, national and local rail and bus enquiry systems
- network ticketing systems, for example, pre-payment systems that are accepted by all local transport providers
- transport interchanges that link road and rail services and, where this is not the case, easy to access links for passengers
- a safer transport system, particularly for those who feel intimidated when using certain forms of public transport
- services that connect in a better, more explicit way to reduce passenger waiting times.

For freight users, similar principles can apply. For example, in order to promote the greater use of rail freight, businesses need to be more aware of the opportunities that are available. There is also a need for more accessible purpose-built freight interchanges such as those that have been built at Doncaster and Daventry over the past few years.

Looking more strategically, a truly integrated transport policy needs to go even further than just public transport and freight use. It has to include road transport and how road users pay to use it. Although rather vague, it was clear from the consultation document that the government were seriously considering road pricing schemes, increasing taxes on company cars and allowing local authorities to charge for city centre car parking places.

Mention was also made of measures to make greater use of bicycles and walking. Overall, this was an obvious commitment to a transport policy that was more integrated than in the past.

From principles to practice – a 'New Deal' for transport

In July 1998, the government's aims for transport policy were set out in the 'New Deal for Transport – Better for Everyone' white paper. Its main points are detailed below. In line with the general objectives for its transport policy, the new deal provided a major boost for public transport, especially with regard to buses. This was a very clear signal that the deregulation of local bus services had not achieved what had been expected (see Chapter 4).

The 'New Deal' for transport policy was also significant in so far as it set up new structures to help meet its objectives. These included:

- A new Strategic Rail Authority, which was charged with promoting the increased use of rail transport and of overseeing operational aspects of the privatisation process, in particular the allocation of passenger franchises. (This body has, however, been short-lived, as explained in Chapter 4.)
- Local Quality Partnerships for bus and freight transport, whereby local government, providers and consumers of transport could meet to tackle various local problems and issues. (The success of these partnerships has, however, been patchy.)
- A Commission for Integrated Transport. This independent body was tasked with providing advice to the government on all transport issues. (It has produced a series of wide-ranging reports, which have not always been supportive of current government policies.)

Significantly, the Transport Act (1998) that followed the 'New Deal' white paper gave local authorities new powers to be able to charge road users for access into major towns and cities (see Chapter 5). This was in line with the earlier commitment to integration and a more environmentally sustainable transport system. This latter and more recent feature of transport policy will be analysed in detail in the following section.

'A New Deal for Transport' – main points

For car drivers:

- increased taxes of £1 billion by 2005, including city centre access charges, workplace parking levies and charges to enter popular countryside areas
- pilot motorway charging schemes

hypothecation of additional taxes to public transport improvement. In simple terms, this means that the money raised by, for example, the London Congestion Charge, goes directly into funding other transport improvements. This is the first time that this principle has been agreed by government.

For public transport:

- £300 million of new investment, especially in light rail transit
- improved interchange facilities
- more bus priority schemes
- a national information system
- quality partnerships
- national concessionary fares scheme.

For railways:

- a new Strategic Rail Authority
- £300 million of new investment to add to that from the private sector
- likely tax relief for regular travellers.

For freight transport:

- more incentives to switch from road to rail
- more encouragement to use vehicles with six axles, which results in less wear and tear on the road surface as the load is more evenly distributed
- quality partnerships.

For pedestrians and cyclists:

- more cycle lanes in towns and cities
- experimental schemes to encourage children to walk or cycle to school
- more 'lollipop' persons with greater powers
- campaigners to get motorists to walk for short trips.

Sustainability in transport policy

In 1987, the United Nation's Bruntland Commission defined sustainable development as 'that which meets the needs of the present without compromising the ability of future generations to meet their own needs'. This can only be achieved through policies that provide for the effective protection of the environment and the prudent use of natural resources.

Greenhouse gas emissions are a major cause of climatic change, the biggest challenge to sustainable development. Transport is responsible for around 20 per cent of all greenhouse gas emissions in the UK but unlike other sectors of the economy, the volume emitted has not been falling over time. Some savings have been made by road transport; in contrast, these have been wiped out by the growth in air transport use. (See *How polluting is your flight?*). A sustainable transport policy can be viewed in two ways. Firstly, it is one that seeks to reduce the emissions from transport by introducing measures that promote the use of those modes of transport that are least polluting in these terms. Secondly, it is a policy that seeks to reduce emissions from those modes of transport that are heavy contributors of greenhouse gases. Both of these approaches have been incorporated into transport policies since 1997, albeit from time-to-time with varying degrees of prominence.

How polluting is your flight?

It might be cheap...but it is going to cost the earth. The cut-price air ticket is fuelling a boom that will make countering global warming impossible. The huge surge in mass air travel is becoming one of the biggest causes of climate change...and will make a nonsense of global targets such as the UK's stated aim of cutting CO_2 emissions by 60 per cent by 2050. Based on predicted air transport growth emissions are expected to rise to 1 727 million tons in 2030. This compares with 8.8 million tons in 2000 and 4.6m tons in 1990. Aircraft emissions go straight into the stratosphere and have more than twice the global warming effect of emissions from cars and power stations at ground level. By 2030, aircraft will be responsible for almost one half of Britain's total expected emissions.

Source: The Independent, 28 May 2005 (adaptation)

Table 1 includes are a few examples of the environmental costs per passenger of a return flight from London to various destinations.

Table 1: Environmental costs per passenger of a return flight from London

	Fuel (kg)	Greenhouse gases (kg CO_2)	Equivalent
Paris	35	330	Using Eurostar would release 40 times less global warming pollutants
New York	414	3 863	Equivalent to 700 two hour trips around the city
Athens	250	2 336	Equivalent to a passenger going without heating, lighting, cooking and mechanised transport for 2.75 years
Sydney	250	2 336	Equivalent to driving a Mini around the earth 640 times, or the weight of four Indian elephants

Source: The Independent, 28 May 2005 (adaptation)

Ideally, we should be reducing our demand for transport or at least cutting back on the rate of increase in demand for transport over time. In practice neither is easy, given the derived demand for transport (see Chapter 1). There is though, much that can be done to switch demand to those modes of transport that generate less greenhouse gas emissions in relation to the volume of demand. For passenger transport:

- The most obvious change would be to reduce dependence on the private car, particularly for short trips where the journey can be made on foot or by bicycle. Around a quarter of all trips made by car are less than a mile in length, including trips to school and college.

- Encouraging greater use of local bus services. This was, after all, the objective of deregulation. The problem we face is that in many places the quality of bus service provision is poor and clearly seen as inferior to the convenient door-to-door service that only a car can provide. The need therefore, is for transport policy to work with operators to make services more attractive, providing real choice for car users.

- Upgrading public transport, in cities especially, by providing more light rail transit systems and other innovative forms of transport. This was one of the aims of the 'Transport 2010' 10-year plan (see page 103 for details).

- Switching demand from road to rail for all types of trip. To some extent, this has occurred with ever-increasing road congestion and through improvements to rail since privatisation. More though, can be achieved, particularly through increased investment in rail infrastructure.

What can economics do?

Economics holds the key to tackling transport problems. Transport policy can bring about changes through:

- Directing transport investment by central and local government to those modes of transport that are more sustainable, for example, light rail systems in cities and upgrading the national railway network. The implication is that road expenditure should be reduced.
- Adjusting the price to transport users to reflect the true cost. This of course is the objective of road user charging (see Chapter 5). Of all policy measures available, this has proven to be the most effective in reducing demand and hence, emissions.
- Technological solutions through passing regulations to reduce CO_2 emissions from vehicles. This has happened and the benefits will progressively occur over time as older vehicles are replaced.
- Increasing the price of fuel in real terms. This was used in the early years of the Labour government but abandoned following the fuel protests of September 2000.

Sustainability in freight transport

For freight transport, the government has sought to make the ways in which goods are moved more sustainable through various measures including:

- making it easier for even more freight to switch from road to rail transport, for both domestic and international traffic
- increasing the maximum weight limit for goods vehicles (see Chapter 2): heavier lorries can carry more freight, meaning less vehicle movements and hence a reduction in CO_2 emissions
- reducing the amount of empty running: about 30 per cent of all goods vehicles' movements are vehicles that are carrying no load. This is a waste of resources so anything a firm can do to reduce empty running will result in cost savings
- better fuel management to reduce waste; again the answer lies with distribution businesses – vehicle routing and scheduling software can often help to improve efficiency
- changes in the way in which vehicles are taxed to make it more expensive for haulers to run trucks that are the least environmentally acceptable and relatively cheap to operate vehicles that are more environmentally friendly.

Most of these possibilities rest with individual firms although the government can use the taxation system to help make the freight function more sustainable.

Another important approach which has far-reaching implications is to raise awareness of how food items are moved within the food supply chain (see Figure 2). There is a growing groundswell of opinion that more could be

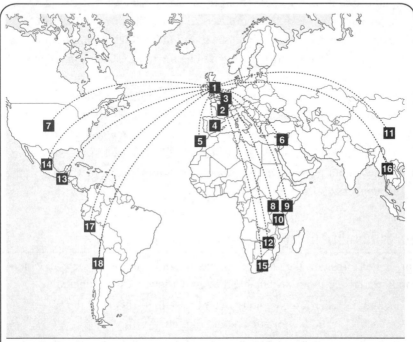

1 Britain
Mushrooms, carrots, sprouts, cauliflower, onions, parsnips, potatoes
2 France
Mushrooms, butternut squash, potatoes, 200 miles
3 Holland
Carrots, peppers, 200 miles
4 Spain
Raspberries, strawberries, fennel, lettuce, tomatoes, cucumber, aubergine, broccoli, marrow, 800 miles
5 Morocco
Sweetcorn, 1300 miles
6 Israel
Radishes, 2200 miles
7 United States
Sweet potatoes, 3700 miles
8 Uganda
Chillies, 4000 miles

9 Kenya
Baby leeks, mangetout, 4200 miles
10 Tanzania
Pak choi, fine beans, 4600 miles
11 China
Ginger, 5100 miles
12 Zimbabwe
Runner beans, 5200 miles
13 Guatemala
Sugar snap peas, 5400 miles
14 Mexico
Red spring onions, 5500 miles
15 South Africa
Grapes, 5600 miles
16 Thailand
Baby sweetcorn, 5900 miles
17 Peru
Asparagus, 6300 miles
18 Chile
Cherries, blueberries, 7200 miles

Figure 2: How far has your food travelled?

done to encourage consumers and retailers to 'think local' when purchasing food items. In this way, the amount of so-called food miles could be reduced and with it, the energy that is being used in supplying our needs. Shoppers and the power of the large supermarkets present an obstacle in so far as we have come to expect all year round availability of goods that at one time were seasonal products. A typical example is strawberries: at one time these were seen as being a special product that was only available for a few weeks in June and July – now they are available all year round. Even when local produce is available, the power of the supermarkets is such that supplies are still imported.

'Transport 2010' – the 10-year plan

In July 2000, the government published a 10-year plan for transport that was, at the time, seen as the means for implementing the strategy analysed in the last two sections. To use a cooking analogy, it was the recipe for putting together the ingredients of an integrated transport policy with the 'New Deal' initiatives to form a coherent transport policy covering the next 10 years.

Its stated objectives were reducing congestion, better integration, better choice and environmental improvement. All were entirely consistent with what has been described earlier. Two important new means of delivery were also included. These were:

- **Public–private partnerships**, mainly to provide funding for the plan's requirements. As Table 2 shows, a massive £180 billion investment and expenditure was projected over the period to 2010. Of this, almost three quarters (£132 billion) was expected to be funded from the public purse. For the private sector, by far the largest sum was to be granted for new railway investment.
- In order to ensure a speedy and efficient delivery of the plan's main features, more emphasis was to be given to local and regional, as opposed to central government, initiatives. This can best be described as a 'bottom up' rather than 'top down' approach.

The plan's main features are detailed below. See also Table 2 for the projected costs.

Table 2: Projected total transport investment and expenditure to 2010/11 (£billion)

	Public investment	Private investment	Total	Public resource spend	Total
Strategic roads	13.6	2.6	16.2	5.0	21.3
Railways	14.7	34.3	49.1	11.3	60.4
Local transport	19.3	9.0	28.3	30.6	58.9
London	7.5	10.4	17.8	7.4	25.3
Other & unallocated	9.7	-	9.7	4.2	13.9
Total	64.7	56.3	121.0	58.6	179.7

Source: DETR, 2000

The main points of the 10-year transport plan

Roads:

- major widening schemes for 360 miles of motorways and trunk roads
- 100 new by-passes
- many local road improvements.

Rail:

- huge capital injection from the public and private sectors to upgrade West Coast, East Coast and Great Western Main Lines
- easing of strategic network bottlenecks in West Midlands and Manchester areas
- new East-West link for London and increase in trans-Pennine capacity
- upgrade of links to deep-sea container ports.

Trams and buses:

- new networks for Leeds, Portsmouth, Bristol and Merseyside and extensions in Birmingham and Manchester; up to 25 new systems in total
- more park and ride schemes and schemes to give priority to buses in urban areas.

A surprising aspect of the plan was the scale of resources being committed to new strategic and local road networks. This seemed to go against the earlier view that the 'predict and provide' approach to transport policy had gone forever. The government's view was that it had underestimated future road congestion and that this level of investment was needed to prevent the situation becoming worse.

This ambitious plan was the first time that a full set of proposals to be implemented had been laid down in this way. For this, the 2010 plan has much to be commended for. On the other hand, since its publication, the plan has been fraught with problems and it is now agreed that the changes detailed above will not all come about. For example, the implementation of local schemes and projects on the national road network has been very slow. Some schemes will not now progress for the following reasons:

- the costs of rail infrastructure improvements have escalated – a very good example is the cost of improving and upgrading the West Coast Main Line
- the private sector has been slow to put money into railways and roads (see Chapter 3)
- most of the planned new light rail systems have run into cost escalation problems and will not be constructed.

This is a very disappointing assessment. It is against this context that the most recent transport policy consultation document, 'The Future of Transport', has been produced.

'The Future of Transport' white paper

The most recent review of transport policy in the UK was published in July 2004. As its name suggests, 'The Future of Transport' is a forward-looking analysis of our transport needs over the next 25 years. Despite the problems of implementation of the 10-year plan (see above), this latest strategic policy document builds upon the progress that has been made since the 10-year plan's implementation.

'The Future of Transport' document firmly recognises the challenge that the country is facing in meeting the future transport needs of people, business and the economy. For example, as the economy grows in the future, the demand for travel will increase. With this, there will be a continuation of the trend for people to travel further for work and leisure reasons. Another challenge is that the population is expected to grow by around 5 million over the next generation. All in all, therefore, meeting transport needs will be essential for national prosperity. This presents a huge challenge for a transport system that is struggling to cope with current, let alone an increasing, demand.

It is this recognition that the demand for transport will continue to increase in the future that is undoubtedly the main feature underpinning this latest policy statement. At the same time, the need to improve peoples' quality of life and to reduce the negative environmental effects of increased transport use is recognised. Transport solutions must therefore meet long term economic, social and environmental goals. If this occurs, then the government's view is that transport will be making its contribution to the objectives of a sustainable development strategy (see above). Not all would agree.

The white paper is a very substantial and comprehensive document covering all modes of passenger and freight transport. Its overall strategy for the future concentrates on three themes. These are:

- Sustained long term investment. The problem of past under-investment is recognised. The planned government investment stated in the 10-year plan (see Table 2) has been increased by 2.25 per cent per annum in real terms and guaranteed now until 2015.
- Improvements in transport management. This is a very general strategy that seeks to ensure that there are improvements in the efficiency of transport operations and that better value is being achieved from public sector funding. A wide range of measures is suggested such as increasing road capacity, high occupancy lanes on motorways, reorganising the railways (see Chapter 4), and more powers for local authorities to procure bus services.
- To plan ahead. This is hardly surprising given the nature of the document. What is significant is that it gives as clear support as any policy document has done for the introduction of road pricing (see Chapter 5). Building more roads or simply doing nothing were firmly rejected.

Table 3 provides a summary of the many ways in which the above three pronged strategy for the Future of Transport is to be implemented. It is vital for all concerned that what is being proposed is realised.

Table 3: The Future of Transport – modal approaches

Type of transport	Modal approach
Roads	New capacity but only where environmental and social costs are taken into account. Road pricing to be seriously debated, especially in relation to providing better choices for motorists.
Railways	Government to be responsible for strategy and improving the organisational structure of the industry. A need to improve standards and keep costs under control.
Local transport	More local congestion charging schemes to assist traffic flow, with more reliable bus services to provide real choice. To see walking and cycling as realistic alternatives to car travel for short journeys.
Air transport	To minimise the environmental impact, while ensuring external costs are met. Implementing the airport development strategy (see Chapter 3).
Freight transport	The focus should be on approaches that provide the best sustainable outcomes (see *Sustainability in Freight Transport* on page 101).

It was stressed that these wide-ranging measures could only be achieved through effective decision-making, particularly at a local and regional level, addressing the full social, economic and environmental costs and benefits involved. Partnership between central and local government through Local Transport Plans was seen as the way in which it could all be realised.

Summary

On completion of this chapter, you have learnt:

- what the objectives of transport policy in the UK are
- what is meant by co-ordination and integration in transport policy
- the means that the government uses to secure the best allocation of resources in the transport sector
- what the role of the private sector is in transport policy
- the main requirements for a more sustainable transport policy
- the strategies being pursued by the UK government in its transport policy.

Useful websites:

Department for Transport www.dft.gov.uk

Transport 2000 www.transport2000.org.uk

Transport Info www.transportinfo.org.uk (provides a daily record of transport issues in the news)

Exam-style practice questions

Data response question

War on the car sparks driver rage

Sweeping measures are to be taken throughout Britain to make motoring increasingly difficult and force millions out of their cars and on to public transport. For example:

- Leeds, Bristol, Edinburgh and Cardiff are about to double the number of bus lanes, and to introduce segregated 'busways' and other measures giving buses right of way.

- Aberdeen, Liverpool, Nottingham, Swansea, Birmingham and Norwich are among cities lining up to introduce devices to change traffic lights in favour of buses in the next year.
- London and other cities are preparing to introduce congestion charging.

The initiatives are a desperate measure to curb the increasing congestion that is throttling British cities. Until late 2000, the government tried to discourage car use by imposing higher duty on petrol through the fuel escalator. However in real terms, the cost of motoring is similar to what it was 25 years ago, while bus fares have increased by 80 per cent.

Congestion charging is planned for some UK cities. The hefty £5 charge proposed for cars entering central London has attracted much criticism and is likely to prove unpopular with motorists. Such charges are vital to reduce the enormous costs of congestion.

The Confederation of British Industry reckons that traffic congestion costs the British economy £20 billion a year, and causes further negative externalities through vehicle emissions. Car drivers in large urban areas now spend a third of their time driving at below 5mph, and journeys are getting ever slower. Over the last five years, the speed of traffic in peak periods has fallen by about 20 per cent.

The government estimates that the volume of traffic is set to rise by a fifth in the next 10 years, making it one of the fastest-growing sources of pollution. Curbing the use of the car and increasing the use of public transport is a central plank in the government's plans to meet its targets for reducing emissions of greenhouse gases.

Nigel Humphries, of the pro-car British Drivers' Association, hit out: 'These are negative measures put in deliberately to obstruct the private motorist. The majority of people have little choice about how they travel, and they are being penalised.'

Source: Joanna Walters, The Observer, 26 August 2001 (adapted)

1. a) Using examples from the article, state why traffic congestion is considered to be a negative externality. (2)

    b) Briefly explain how the costs of traffic congestion might be estimated. (4)

c) With the aid of a diagram, comment on the extent to which increased taxes on petrol might discourage car use. (4)

d) Explain the likely reasons why the real cost of bus fares has increased by 80 per cent over the last 25 years. (4)

e) Discuss whether the introduction of congestion charges in major cities is likely to 'force millions out of their cars and on to public transport.' (6)

(OCR, Module 2885, January 2004)

Essay questions

1. a) Explain what is meant by a sustainable transport policy. (10)

   b) Discuss the contribution that road pricing can make to a sustainable transport policy. (15)

(OCR, Module 2885, June 2003)

Examination skills for transport economics

Types of questions

There are two main types of questions that are asked. These are:

- Essay questions. These questions may have one or two parts and provide an opportunity for you to write in length and depth about your knowledge of the subject.
- Data response questions. These questions require only short answers to questions that are drawn from 'data' that may consist of numerical data, text or a combination of both.

General principles

When producing answers in an examination to either type of question, it is important for you to remember the basic skills that are needed for success in any examination. So please remember to:

- allocate your time effectively in relation to the marks available
- write to the point of the question – do not waste time skirting around what is required
- construct your answer in a form that is consistent with the 'directive' word in the question. For example, a question that asks: 'describe what is meant by road pricing' is not the same as one that asks: 'explain what is meant by road pricing' which is different again from one that asks: 'discuss what is meant by road pricing'.

To get good marks, you need to direct your answer in the way that the examiner expects.

Essay questions

Essay questions give you the opportunity to demonstrate to examiners that you have an extensive knowledge of transport economics and that you can evidence this knowledge by writing in a coherent and meaningful way.

A typical essay question might be:

'Discuss the case for user charging as a means of combating traffic congestion in cities.'

A simple structure for your essay is given in the following table:

1st paragraph	Two or three sentences of context, for example, the relevance of user charging in transport policy at the present time.
Body of answer	A series of points including: - a definition of user charging - the case for user charging, for example, as a means of addressing market failure, needed to offset forecast increase in traffic, revenue can be used to improve public transport, has been proven to actually reduce traffic flows - the case against user charging, for example, equity considerations, privacy problems, road tax and fuel tax are much easier to apply, its unpopularity with road users, the problem of charge estimation.
Conclusion	Make the point that there are arguments in favour of and against user charging. Ideally, this should be a balanced assessment.

The structure of what you write is very important – a well-structured essay will usually gain you a good mark. So, spend a few minutes in the examination writing out a simple essay plan such as the one given above.

A few more tips

Many examinations, including OCR's transport economics paper, are assessed by examiners using what is known as a 'level of response' marking scheme. The marks awarded depend upon whether you evidence a particular level of skill in your answer. At A level, the two top levels are for answers which show analysis and evaluation. At the same time though, you must also demonstrate an appropriate grasp of the subject content of the question commensurate with the skill level.

At the top level, examiners are looking for answers that evaluate the topic or issue raised in the question. A clue that this type of answer is needed is if the directive word of the question is 'discuss', 'comment' or 'evaluate'. The word 'discuss' is widely used in OCR examinations and is encouraging you to put two sides of a particular argument. This should be rational and balanced; opinionated answers looking only at one side will not get many marks.

Another useful tip is to write in an analytical way, avoiding tedious, unnecessary description. Questions that have 'analyse' as the directive word have obviously to be answered in this way. Questions that start with the directive word 'explain' should also be tackled in this way. Here a reasoned account is required.

Other useful pieces of advice are:

- Remember to use economics terminology as much as you can. After all, it is an economics examination. Look at the key words in the book and use as many as you can in your answers.

- Diagrams are an essential part of the economist's 'tool kit'. Use a diagram in your answer where this is appropriate. Know the figures in the book as these might be useful. Do not though, include a badly drawn or irrelevant diagram in an answer – this is just a waste of valuable writing time.

- Surprisingly few students ever refer in their answers to things that they have read, whether it be books, newspapers, magazines or something from the Internet. Do this if you can remember – it may gain you another mark.

- Draw upon local examples to add substance to your answer. This could be done for questions on traffic congestion, a new by-pass, bus deregulation and so on.

- Remember to always have a concluding paragraph, particularly to answers that have a large number of marks attached to them.

Data response questions

These questions are much more varied. In all cases, a small number of questions are asked; these are drawn either directly or indirectly from the information that has been provided. It is usual for simple, straightforward questions to be asked in the early parts, moving on to questions that require a few sentences of reasonably detailed explanation or commentary. Simple calculations may also be required.

There are many possible sources of data response questions, including statistical publications such as Transport Statistics of Great Britain, newspapers including search engines, the BBC News website and government publications.

The golden rule in answering all of these questions though is to keep it brief, and where possible, draw upon the information that has been provided.

Where the question contains numerical data:

- Make sure you know what the data means. Look at the units (if any) and whether the data is in a percentage or a raw form.

- Where the data is in the form of a table or diagram, spend a couple of minutes 'eye balling' what is provided. For example, look along the rows or down the columns of data to pick out any trends. This is especially relevant where you are given time series data.

▪ With text, read it through picking out relevant economic terms. These should give you a pointer to the questions that follow.

You should also spend a couple of minutes looking at all of the questions. These follow a logical order. By looking at all of the questions you can avoid a possible situation were you might be writing information in one part of the question when it is really required later on.

The general principles referred to earlier apply but with one important addition – if you cannot answer a particular part of a data response question, move on! Do not waste time when you could be gaining marks elsewhere in the examination.

Worked examples of typical examination questions

Essay question

Many of the essay questions at A level are 'structured' into two related parts. The question below is typical of what you can expect. It draws upon what you have learned in Chapter 4.

1. a) Explain the factors that determine whether a market is
      contestable.   (10)
   b) Drawing upon a transport market of your choice, discuss
      whether this market is contestable at the present time.   (15)

Advice on what is required

First impressions – the content of this question is central to understanding the concept of deregulation and its application to transport markets. Part b) is clearly more challenging than part a) as it is looking for application and evaluation, although it does provide you with every opportunity to write about a market that particularly interests you and is known to you.

Now see if you can answer the question, before looking at the suggested response.

Part a) is asking you to provide a reasoned account of whether a market may or may not be contestable. No application is required. You must use as much economics terminology as you can, taking care to say 'why' particular characteristics of a contestable market are relevant.

Broadly speaking contestability is a concept that is used to explain how, within any market structure, it is possible for any firm, large or small, to realistically compete with any other firm on a fair basis. The characteristics or features of a perfectly contestable market are outlined on pages 53–54.

To get good marks, two key points should be stressed. These are:

- Free, costless entry and exist.
- A pool of potential entrants waiting to get into the market if the behaviour of existing firms indicates that more competition is needed. The size of firm should not matter.

If these are present then the market will be contestable. Barriers to entry are particularly important in real world markets. This should be stressed. A very good answer could also refer to the other characteristics of a contestable market.

The answer to this part should be clear and concise, written in an analytical style with an emphasis on explanation.

A good mark for part b) requires you to have:

- A competent understanding of a transport market that is known to you.
- The ability to compare the reality of this market with the conceptual characteristics that you referred to in your answer to part a).

If you have no knowledge outside this book, do not worry. Chapter 4 provides examples drawn from bus and rail transport in Great Britain, and low cost airlines and logistics operations in Europe. These will help, although you must make sure your knowledge is reasonably up-to-date to meet the 'at the present time' requirement of the question. Alternatively, knowledge of a local market may be useful.

A good approach is to consider barriers to entry and how and why these restrict the entry of new firms into your chosen market. In some transport markets such as rail and air, barriers to entry are very high; in local bus and road freight transport markets they are by no means as restrictive. In all markets though, it is difficult to envisage a situation where there is costless entry and exit.

On the basis of the evidence you have produced, your final paragraph should be an effective discussion of the extent to which your chosen market is contestable. As a guide, over time few, if any, transport markets are as contestable as they were when they were deregulated. However, in most markets there are still opportunities for new firms, although these are usually on a niche market basis only due to the force of competition from incumbent firms.

A word of warning: if you do not discuss the issues involved, the maximum marks you will be awarded are nine out of the 15 that are available.

Data response question

Study the information below and then answer the questions that follow.

The real cost of transport in the UK

Over the past 25 years or so, personal disposable income in the UK has increased at a steady rate. Simultaneously, there has been an almost continuous increase in the demand for personal travel. Between 1980 and 2004:

- Transport by private car increased by 83 per cent.
- Bus and coach transport declined over the same period, except in London where it increased by 60 per cent on the 1980 level.
- Rail travel declined up to privatisation in the mid-1990s but then increased quite significantly.

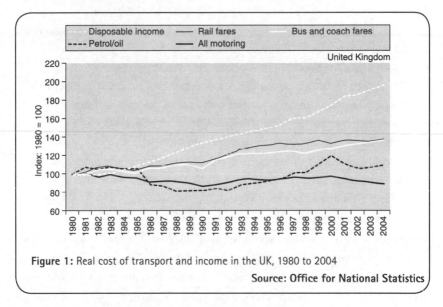

Figure 1: Real cost of transport and income in the UK, 1980 to 2004

Source: Office for National Statistics

It is widely believed that the real cost of transport is the most important consideration in determining an individual's demand for a particular mode of transport. Figure 1 below shows the changes in the real cost of personal transport and in income from 1980 to 2004.

1. Define:
   a) disposable income
   b) real cost of transport. (2)

2. Use Figure 1 to describe the relationship between disposable income and the real cost of transport over the period 1980 to 2004. (4)

3. State and explain two possible reasons why public transport (rail, bus and coach) costs have increased more than motoring costs. (4)

4. Use the information in Figure 1 to comment on whether it is more affordable to run a car in 2004 than in 1980. (4)

5. Discuss the extent to which 'the real cost of transport' is the most important consideration in determining an individual's demand for a particular mode of transport. (6)

Advice on what is required

First impressions – the concepts contained in the question are some that you have come across in Chapter 1, Table 2 and Figure 3 especially, although the way in which these concepts are presented is different.

Scanning the text and 'eye balling' the data should indicate that:

- There are two important economic terms used: 'real cost' and 'disposable income'. Think about what each means.
- Figure 1 is a time series. Think about the time scale involved.
- The data in Figure 1 is shown in index form. This makes it quite easy to compare the trend in one variable with that in another variable.
- Disposable income has nearly doubled over the period shown. People are much better off in 2004 than they were in 1980.
- Motoring costs do not appear to have risen at all in these terms; public transport fares have increased well above the cost of motoring.

Now that these basics have been established, try to answer the questions yourself, before going on to look at the suggested responses.

Question 1 – there are only two marks available, one for each definition. You must therefore be concise and clear in what you write. You need to recall what these terms mean from elsewhere in your A Level course – they are not specific terms just for transport economics.

Disposable income – this is income that remains once direct taxes and other earnings related payments have been deducted. More simply, it is income a person has available to spend.

Real cost of transport – 'real' is the key word and is used to denote a situation where the effects of inflation have been taken into account. So the real cost of transport is the cost of transport adjusted for inflation.

Question 2 – this type of question is widely used in time series data response questions. It requires you to compare two of the trends in Figure 1. Data regurgitation is not required, only a broad indication with some statement of the time period involved. This is important. Note the question says real cost of 'transport' – you can therefore refer to three of the entries in the time series (not petrol/oil).

Possible responses are:

- Since 1985, disposable income has increased at a faster rate than the real cost of any of the three modes of transport (up to 1985, the relationship was not as clear).
- For the period as a whole, disposable income has increased by about 90 per cent while motoring costs have remained stable.
- The gap between the increase in disposable income and rail fares is least when taken over the whole period.
- The change in real transport costs has been more volatile than the change in disposable income over the period.

Four marks are available. Any two of the above points should get you full marks. A common mistake with this type of question is that students try to explain why the trend has occurred. This is beyond the scope of the question.

Question 3 – this is another common format of data response question. It requires you to simply 'state' a reason and then add a few words to 'explain' the choice you have made. The use of the word 'possible' in the question indicates that you do not need explicit knowledge; in other words, the examiner is prepared to accept anything that seems to be logical economics.

To answer this question, you need to think about what constitutes the main costs of the various modes of transport. Possible reasons could be:

- Wages of bus drivers and railway workers have increased above the rate of inflation.
- Less subsidies have been paid to bus and rail operators so fares have had to increase.
- Excessive profits are being earned by the privatised operators of bus and rail services.
- The retail price of new and used cars has fallen in real terms; cost of buses and operating rail services has increased in real terms.
- Road taxes, excluding petrol taxes, have fallen in real terms.

There are plenty of possible answers, but remember to be brief as only four marks are available for two different reasons.

Question 4 – this question is more challenging. You have to consider the data in Figure 1 and make a 'comment'. It is also important that you appreciate what 'affordable' means, that is, the cost of running a car in relation to income.

So, remembering that disposable income has almost doubled while motoring costs have remained the same over the period, you can deduce:

- It is more affordable to run a car in 2004 than in 1980. This statement alone should get one mark.
- The change in disposable income is much greater than the change in motoring costs. This explanation should get one more mark.

The 'comment' aspect is trickier. Any one of the points below with a little reasoning should get you two more marks. For example:

- As disposable income increases, one of the first things people tend to buy is a car (if they do not already own one).
- The data does not take into account the external costs of using a car.
- The data assumes motoring costs are the same for any type of car. However, as incomes increase, the tendency for many people is to buy a more expensive car.
- Rail users may decide to buy a car due to the real increase in their travel costs compared with motoring costs.

Question 5 – this question is more open-ended and is drawn from a sentence in the information that has been provided. The 'discuss the extent' directive is a very clear indication that you must look at both sides of this particular problem. You should raise the respective issues involved and, if you feel confident, state whether you feel the real cost of transport really is the most important consideration in determining an individual's demand for a particular mode of transport.

The background to this question is also in Chapter 1 where it was stated that the demand for a given mode of transport is dependent on:

- price (i.e. the real cost of that mode of transport)
- price of substitutes (i.e. the real cost of other modes of transport)
- income
- quality variables.

These are of course the usual determinants of demand for any product or service. Looking again at the question, it is asking: 'how important is price relative to the other three variables?' A good approach therefore, is to direct your answer in this way.

The question is also inviting you to look at it from the perspective of 'a particular mode of transport'. Taking the private car as an example:

- Quality variables such as convenience, flexibility and door-to-door service tend to be very important as to why someone uses a car. The real cost is perhaps less of a consideration.

- For higher income earners, most will have a car available, and will use it.
- The higher real cost of public transport may not be an issue for most regular car users.

A final sentence that explains the extent to which the real cost is most important is likely to impress, provided of course your underpinning arguments are reasonable. A failure to enter into a discussion will give you no more than two marks out of the six available.

Conclusion

Much has happened in transport since the 3rd edition of *Transport Economics* was published in 2001. Notably:

- the successful implementation of congestion charging in London and a commitment by the government to introduce a radical system of national road user charging
- the opening of the M6 Toll Road, the first major privately-funded road scheme in the UK
- important structural changes to the organisation of railways, a consequence of the collapse of Railtrack and the abolition of the Strategic Rail Authority
- the continued spectacular growth of low-fare airlines, alongside confirmation as to how the UK's airport capacity will be expanded to meet increased demand
- huge amounts of capital being committed to expanding the capacity of the most congested parts of the road network
- increased subsidy being paid to train operating companies
- serious doubts over whether the government remains committed to a more sustainable transport policy.

These are just some of the topics covered in this book. A common thread that holds these topics together is that all of them, in some form or another, are indicative of resource allocation problems. It is the function of economics to put forward outcomes as to how resource allocation might be improved. Furthermore, it is the role of economists to put theories into practice through the development and realisation of appropriate transport policies.

Readers should remember that the book is a snapshot of transport at a point in time. Transport is an ever-changing sector – the list of useful websites will help you to keep up-to-date.

Finally, I hope that this book has stimulated your interest in transport economics and transport issues. For some readers, I further hope that it may have provided a basis for future study and possibly a challenging career in this vitally important sector of the economy.

Index

accidents 19, 21–2, 23, 39–40, 43, 63
air transport 6, 7, 9, 44, 45
    costs 17, 19, 30–1, 99–100
    environmental impact 19, 26,
        31, 45, 99–100, 106
airlines 17, 31, 33, 60–2, 70
    low-fare 7, 17, 26, 44–5, 52, 60,
        61, 62, 120
airports 29–31, 44–7, 60, 61, 76, 106,
    120
    investment 33, 34, 47
    privatisation 33, 45, 62

barriers to entry 17, 50, 51–2, 53, 55,
    68, 74
bus transport 4, 5, 10, 12, 58, 82, 104,
    107–8
    deregulation 10, 52, 55–9, 74,
        96, 97, 100
    fares 6, 8, 28, 57, 59, 108
    London 9, 12, 28, 52, 56, 58–9,
        74
    subsidies 28, 28–9, 57

carbon dioxide see emissions
cars see private cars
CO$_2$ see emissions
commuting 39, 41, 71
competition 50–5, 74, 94
    rail industry 67–8, 70
congestion 9, 18, 19, 36, 63, 76–8,
    83–5, 91
    combating 36–8, 40, 82–3, 104
    costs 22, 23, 39, 78–81, 108
    increase in 12, 31, 95, 108

congestion charging 83, 84, 86, 90,
    97, 106, 108
    London 28, 83, 84, 85, 86, 120
contestable markets 52–3, 53–5, 55,
    60, 68, 74
cost-benefit analysis 21, 38–47
costs 16–18, 20, 22, 29, 101
    accidents 19, 21–2, 23, 39–40
    congestion 22, 23, 39, 78–81
    environmental 18, 22, 23, 24,
        99–100
    external 18, 20, 22–4, 78–80
    social 18, 20, 45, 47
    user costs 30–41, 00
cycling 5, 26, 97, 98, 100, 106

demand 4–8, 10–12, 14, 25, 44, 100,
    105–6
deregulation 33, 53, 55, 93
    bus services 10, 52, 55–9, 74,
        96, 97, 100
    EU air services 60–2, 74

efficiency 20, 54, 57, 63, 70
emissions 19, 43, 46, 99, 101
    air transport 26, 99–100
    congestion 76, 79, 108
    food transport 23, 24
environmental costs 18, 22, 23, 24,
    99–100
EU (European Union) 59–60, 60–2, 74,
    77–8, 91
examination skills 110–19
external costs 18, 20, 22, 78–80
externalities 18–24, 27, 29, 35, 42,
    78, 108

fares 6, 7, 8, 28, 57, 59, 98, 108
   rail 6, 7, 8, 68–70, 71, 72
food miles 23–4, 102–3
franchising 28, 52, 56, 58–9
   rail 6, 63, 65, 66, 67–8, 68, 71, 97
freight transport 6, 7–8, 9, 10–12, 15, 50, 96, 97, 98
   air 44
   rail 10, 66, 67, 68, 96, 98
   sustainability 11, 101–3, 106
   see also food miles; logistics
fuel 25, 40, 58, 76, 101
   taxes 22, 25, 28, 78, 87, 91, 108
Future of Transport, The (DfT, 2004) 12, 93, 105–7

government 4, 8, 120
   investment 47, 71–2, 94, 101, 103, 104, 106
   spending 13, 24, 33, 36, 72
greenhouse gases see emissions

indirect taxation 24–7, 29, 45, 78, 91
infrastructure 3, 8, 33, 34–5, 65, 66, 68, 100, 105
integrated transport 42, 43, 107
   policy 43, 95–7, 103
investment 33–6, 47, 68, 100, 106
   rail 44, 68, 71, 73, 103
   see also private sector; public sector

logistics 59–60, 81
London
   airports 29–31, 45, 46, 47, 61, 76
   buses 9, 12, 28, 56, 58–9, 74
   congestion charge 28, 83, 84, 85, 86, 120

lorries 8, 17, 40–1, 98, 101
low-fare airlines 7, 17, 26, 44–5, 52, 60, 61, 62, 120
LRUC (Lorry Road User Charge) 90–1

M6 Toll Road 33, 35, 38, 120
market failures 29, 47, 83–5, 86, 91
market structures 50–3, 74
monopolies 50, 51, 52, 53, 56, 63, 64–5, 68–70

negative externalities 18–24, 29, 35, 42, 78, 108
New Deal for Transport (DfT, 1998) 97–8, 103
noise 19, 22, 23, 42, 43, 79

passenger transport 4, 6, 9, 10, 11–12, 50
PFI (Private Finance Initiative) 33, 35–6
pollution 19, 22, 23, 26, 43, 63
   air transport 26, 99–100
   see also emissions; noise
prices 6, 27, 36, 54, 68–70, 101
private cars 4, 5, 9, 10, 12, 18–19, 78, 100
   costs 6, 7, 8, 17, 108
private costs 17, 17–18, 20, 29
Private Finance Initiative (PFI) 33, 35–6
private sector 4, 8–10, 14, 33, 56, 105, 107
   investment 33, 35–6, 47, 73, 103, 104, 105
privatisation 33, 45, 55–6, 62–3, 74, 93, 94
   rail 10, 63–73, 74, 97
public sector 32, 36, 38, 63, 93
   investment 47, 71–2, 94, 101, 103, 104, 106

public transport 5, 82, 91, 97, 98, 100, 108

rail transport 4, 5, 6, 7, 9, 17, 19, 104, 106
  benefits 43, 63
  commuting 71
  demand 10
  fares 6, 7, 8, 68–70, 71, 72
  franchising 6, 63, 65, 66, 67–8, 68, 71, 97
  freight 10, 66, 67, 68, 96, 98
  improvements 100, 101
  infrastructure 8, 33, 34, 65, 66, 68, 100, 105
  investment 33, 34, 43–4, 68, 71, 72, 73, 100, 103
  organisation 66, 101, 120
  privatisation 10, 63–73, 74, 97
  safety 72–3, 73
  subsidies 4, 6, 28, 43, 64, 65, 68, 82, 120
resource allocation 18, 20, 32–6, 47, 63, 93, 107, 120
road pricing 25, 82–90, 91, 96, 97, 106, 120
road transport 5, 9, 10, 12–13, 17, 19, 95–6, 108
roads 8, 36, 82, 104, 106, 120
  appraisal of schemes 21, 38–43
  building 42, 82, 91, 106
  cost-benefit analysis 38–42
  costs 22, 23–4, 38, 78–80
  expenditure 22, 24, 36, 101
  improvements 36–8, 104, 120
  investment 33, 34

safety 43, 72–3, 73
  see also accidents

social benefits 42, 45, 47
social costs 18, 20, 45, 47
subsidies 4, 27–9, 47, 57, 65
  rail 4, 6, 28, 43, 64, 65, 68, 82, 120
supply chains 3, 4, 7–8, 9, 13, 59–60, 102–3
sustainability 10, 11–12, 101–3, 106
sustainable transport policy 45, 95, 98–100, 101, 107, 120

taxation 20, 31, 86, 98, 101–2
  fuel taxes 22, 25, 28, 31, 78, 87, 91, 108
  indirect 24–7, 29, 45, 78, 91
  road users 22, 87, 96, 97–8
traffic forecasts 12–13, 14
transport 3–13, 14, 100, 105–6
  costs 16–18, 29
  integration 42, 43, 107
  management 91, 106
Transport 2010 (DfT, 2000) 33, 100, 103–5
transport markets 29, 49–55, 74
transport policy 13, 43, 73, 93–8, 101, 103–7, 120
  sustainability in 45, 95, 98–100, 101–3, 106, 107
true costs 18, 22, 29, 101

UK (United Kingdom) 13, 36–8, 44–7, 63–73, 77–8, 106, 120
user charging 83, 84, 101
user costs 38–41, 80

value of time costs 39, 41, 80

walking 4, 5, 97, 98, 100, 106